The following articles appeared in my syndicated column

From the Kitchen Table

between 2009 and 2012

Higher Authority

Today, everyone is quoting the Founding Fathers. The words of Thomas Jefferson, John Adams, George Washington, and Benjamin Franklin, to name just a few, are appearing in newspaper articles, Internet blogs, and radio commentaries. But for those who lived in the turbulent years between 1760 and 1785, it was the words of others who actually moved the opinion of the public to support the efforts of their more famous political counterparts.

Those others were pastors. And they spoke in the pulpits of the American colonies – passionately and eloquently defending the ideas expressed in the American Declaration. Men like Jonathan Mayhew, John Wesley, Moses Mather, John Witherspoon, Richard Price, Jonathan Edwards, and Noah Webster, who used the voice of the church to explain why tyranny was indefensible, and how King George's actions constituted tyranny.

As America grew, the churches were not silent bystanders.

They spoke, often and clearly, about the issues confronting this nation. They spoke against corruption, no matter what office the corruption arose from. They spoke about the need for diligence in protecting America's freedoms. They called attention to injustice, and demanded its correction.

Their input reminded everyone, government official and citizen alike, that there is an authority higher than the state. An authority to which all are equally accountable. An authority that does not bend with the political winds, but judges by unchanging standards of right and wrong.
But in 1954, then Senator Lyndon Johnson orchestrated the addition of language to the IRS tax codes. The language said that, for the first time in American history, the churches were to be silent on issues that were "political". A church that dared to speak out would be punished.

Under the 1954 standards, every single one of the sermons delivered in support of the work of our Founding Fathers would be considered illegal.

What happened?

The answer it both simple and frightening.

Government grew, and it wants to keep growing – in power and in size.

And for government to continue its growth, it must silence any voice that reminds the citizens that there should be a limit to the authority of the state. The church is pre-eminent among those voices because the church, by definition, represents the REAL ultimate authority. The denomination does not really matter in the eyes of the state – no matter what name a particular religion gives to that authority figure, every religion is based on the premises that 1) this authority exists and 2) it is higher than the government.

No government intent on growth can tolerate this. So as the government grows, so does the hostility to the church.

Today we not only have a ban on church speech, but some elected officials even insist that churches cover any religious symbol on their own property if a government program or person is in attendance. After all, that symbol might remind someone that the government is accountable to Someone.

The fact that the government worries so much about silencing the churches seems ridiculous. After all, no pastor commands an army, and no local Reverend can actually change any vote or remove any official just by speaking about it from a pulpit. No citizen has to join a church, or attend its services. And any pastor will tell you that those who do attend do not listen to and heed his words every time – response is purely voluntary.

But whether an individual responds or not, the voice of the church is a constant reminder that government is not the ultimate authority, and should have limits. It's a voice that needs to be protected.

The Taxman Cometh

Among the sneakiest things the government has done was institute a withholding tax system, and make some taxes "employer taxes".

The withholding system makes taxes invisible to most citizens. When one asks a taxpayer how much they will pay this year, the most common answer is a smiling declaration of how big a refund is coming. Most of us have no idea how much we actually paid in taxes – even though it is written on our pay stubs. And most taxpayers also have no understanding of the fact that if they ARE getting a refund, it is because they gave the government an interest-free loan in the amount of that refund.

Let's take just one example to analyze how much we actually paid this year. We will use an average salary of $35,000. A worker making $35,000 will pay $2,677.50 in Social Security and Medicare taxes, which are not subject to refund no matter what deductions he has. He will pay $1,074.50 in Pennsylvania state income tax. He will pay $31.50 in state unemployment tax. If he is lucky enough to live in a low-tax municipality, he will pay $350.00 in local income taxes, but if he lives in Philadelphia, he will pay $1,375.50. He will also pay $1.00 per week in Local Services Tax, or $52.00 each year.

So the payroll tax burden, <u>before the federal income tax,</u> on an individual in Pennsylvania who makes just $35,000 lies between $4,185.50 and $5,211.00. But since every one of these taxes is collected through payroll deduction, most of us don't really pay attention. And that inattention is exactly why the government likes the withholding system.
But that is only part of the tax puzzle. The employer side must by calculated as well. This side is truly invisible to most employees because it never appears on a paycheck.

It works like this.

When a business decides to hire an employee, the business owner figures out how much he can afford in a salary package. Part of that package is the tax burden the business will incur by hiring that employee.

If the business can afford a package of $38,000, it can only give $35,000 of that in salary because it will need to give the government $2,677.50 in employer Social Security and Medicare taxes, $434.00 in federal unemployment taxes, and between $175.48 and $1,133.70 in state unemployment tax.

So an employer must pay from $38,286.98 to $39,245.20 – without counting the accounting costs of doing all the government's paperwork, or the cost of health care or regulations, to give an employee $35,000 in salary.

If we add those numbers together, the payroll taxes – without federal income tax – for one worker who makes $35,000 a year are between a possible low of $7,482.48 and a possible high of $9,456.20. And every penny of it is withheld ahead of time.

If we really want to hold government accountable for its spending, the best first step is to eliminate withholding, so every American has to actually write the checks. When people are aware of how much they are really paying, they will be much more likely to begin asking what they are paying for.

Support and Defend

We have parades and speeches. We attend memorial services.
We watch reruns of war movies. We may even buy a veteran or
a current member of our armed forces a beer. Our annual
celebration of Veteran's Day is pretty predictable.

And when we are done, we feel good – about our military, and
about ourselves for honoring them each year.

We shouldn't.

Because parades and memorials and movies and small gifts really
don't have anything to do with honoring the sacrifice America's
veterans made.   To actually honor the sacrifice we need to
recognize, and contribute to, the reason for their service.

Let's start with our first American veterans. They were standing
against the mightiest empire in their world in a fight that no one
believed they could win.   There was no glory in Valley Forge.
The soldiers who wintered there were starving, and freezing, and
even bleeding. Observers at the time said that one could follow
each sentry's route by tracking his bloody footprints through the
snow.

Those men didn't know that they would win. They did know that
the principles of liberty they were fighting for were worth the
sacrifice they were making. Even if that sacrifice was their very
lives.

Those principles were embodied in the United States
Constitution. And every generation of America's military has
sworn to support and defend that Constitution so those principles
remain intact. That means that our military pledges allegiance to
a structure of government that guarantees the freedom of every
American citizen.

And in the over 200 years of our existence, many of them have honored that pledge at the cost of their lives.

We are the citizens whose freedom they protect.

And when we do not value that freedom, we dishonor their gift.

In the election last week, voter turnout in Pennsylvania was 21%. The declared winner was "voter apathy".

That is a slap in the face of every man or woman who has ever worn the uniform. They stand in front of bullets to protect the rights of citizens who can't be bothered to show up to vote.

The same Constitution that they pledge to support and defend places the responsibility for America's government in the hands of America's citizens. The ballot box gives citizens the opportunity to completely change the makeup of the United States House of Representatives every 2 years. It's the ability to stage a revolution without firing a single shot.

Our Founders understood how truly terrible bloody revolutions would be. So they gave us a structure of government that enabled us to "revolt" without having to endure the horrors of war. And they gave us a military that was pledged to protect that structure.

They could do no more. Using the Constitution's structure to protect our American freedoms is our job as American citizens.

This Veteran's Day, let's truly honor the men and women who have protected our structure of freedom. Let's resolve that we will do our part to support and defend the Constitution of the United States by becoming informed and active participants in every election. It's the least that we can do in appreciation for their service.

Practicality

Today is Good Friday. On this day, Christians around the world will gather to commemorate the most impractical act a man ever committed. On this day, one man chose to die so countless others, many of whom would not even know His name, could have life.

In each of the events leading up to 3:00 PM, the people making the controlling decisions told themselves that they were being practical.

Judas went to the high priests because he believed that Christ was not being practical with money.

The high priests believed that it was more practical for one man to die than to possibly incur the wrath of the Roman Empire.

Pontius Pilate gave into the demands of the crowd for crucifixion because he believed that it was more practical to sacrifice Christ than to have civil unrest.

The disciples ran away because they believed that there was no practical way to stay faithful and avoid death themselves, and there was no practical reason for them to die.

There were a few impractical folks that day. Folks who cared more about the man being tortured and killed than they did about any practical considerations.

We know their names as well. Veronica, who impractically stepped into the path of the soldiers and the screaming mob to wipe His bleeding face. Mary Magdalene, who impractically braved the jeers of the soldiers to remain faithful to her Lord. Mary, his mother, who impractically followed her Son all the way to the foot of the cross so He could see and take comfort from her loving presence. John, who impractically stood in the middle of the Golgotha nightmare, living up to the term "beloved disciple".

And now it is two thousand years later, and we are about to commemorate the events of that day. In our discussions, we don't often use the word "practical" to describe the actions of those who contributed to the death. We use other, uglier, adjectives. We also don't use the word "impractical" to describe the actions of the few who remained by His side. We use other words there as well.

It's funny how often practicality is called a virtue in the present tense, and a vice in the past tense.

That's because most of us would not openly embrace a choice that we know is unprincipled. We all like to see ourselves as individuals who "do the right thing". But doing the right thing is often hard. It may cost us financially. It may mean less prestige. It may end a relationship. It may make our path more difficult. It may result in a perceived failure.

So we convince ourselves that we can sacrifice principle for practicality. We tell ourselves that we would prefer to do the principled thing, but it just wouldn't be practical to do so this time.

On this day, when we remember the impractical Man who embraced a cross for us, let's take just a moment to consider all the times that we chose practicality over principle. And then let's remember which of the people who were in Jerusalem on this day two thousand years ago made that same choice, and which ones did not.
If we truly mean to follow the Man whose sacrifice we honor, we need to join the second group. Without exception and without compromise.

Answers

Ask any warden in any juvenile detention center about the single factor that most of the inmates have in common and you will be told that they came from a family without a father.

Talk to those who work with teenage girls who become pregnant and ask them the same question. You will receive the same answer.

Now speak with school guidance counselors about the characteristics of those who drop out. You will hear about children without fathers.

Finally, examine the statistics about children who grow up in conditions of poverty, and you will find a direct correlation between economic level and family structure, with fatherless families at the bottom of the pile.

In fact, for every problem situation involving children, a missing father is the single most common factor.

The government has developed and funded an ever-increasing number of programs to replace the father. The programs have attempted to provide financially for families without fathers through welfare, rent subsidies, and health care. They have created networks for children without fathers, with counselors and facilitators. They have restructured educational and social programs to make allowances for children without fathers at home. The research proves that all of these initiatives don't work. And the negative societal impact of missing fathers continues to grow.

The obvious question is, "Why?"
The answer is almost too uncomplicated to be believable.

Simply put, there is no government substitute for a Dad.

Dads don't just provide for families and children. Dads love them. It doesn't matter whether the child is a girl or a boy, the loving presence of Dad is critical.

Little boys have a hero to look up to and imitate. Dads not only solve problems, they give horsey-back rides and play catch. A mother concentrates on kissing boo-boo's, but a father tells them to try again. And in trying again, the little one learns that a failure is just another step on the way to eventual success.

Adolescent boys learn that limits still apply. They may be bigger than Mom, but they are still not as big, or as strong, as Dad. It is much better to try to push the envelope against Dad than against the legal establishment. Adult men often share laughing stories of how they thought they could "show Dad" when they were in their teens, only to discover that Dad "showed" them. And so they learned that the rules still applied to them in a setting where the discipline was tempered with love.

Dads are just as important to girls. It is Dad who first tells his daughter that there is something special about being a girl. It is Dad who sets the standard for how she should expect to be treated by the opposite sex. It is Dad who communicates that standard to the young men she dates. It is Dad who combines an expectation of her excellence with an appreciation of her femininity. And so daughters learn that women can be strong and successful and still enjoy being women. And they learn to expect to be treated courteously and respectfully by every other man because they were treated that way by their fathers.
If we truly want to solve the problems confronting our youth, we should be concentrating on making sure they have the one thing that best meets their needs.

A Dad.

Happy Father's Day!

Removing the Tentacles

Federal government policies almost always reach far beyond their intended consequences, creating problems in areas that their Washington advocates never anticipated. It's like a "Murphy's Law" for citizens – government programs will cause anything that CAN go wrong, TO go wrong, even if the disaster didn't appear to be connected to the program that caused it.

The good news in this picture is that removing the federal government from a situation in an intelligent fashion can reverse the disasters that Washington interference created.

Let's start with energy.

We don't import oil because we don't have any. We import oil because Washington has forbidden the states to drill the oil we have. The same sad reality is true for coal and natural gas. It's like we Americans are sitting before a banquet table loaded with a bountiful feast, and are starving ourselves to death.

But what if we unshackled our energy reserves? What if we told Washington that energy policy was a state issue, and freed the states to develop their energy resources?

The first effect would be economic. Reopening existing coal mines and oil wells and creating new ones would create jobs for the miners or drillers. It would also stimulate all the industries that support those mines or wells. Industries such as timber, rail, metal workers, and foundries would be positively affected. The industries that provide safety and drilling equipment would grow. And growth in industry means growth in the job market, with jobs that don't depend on the next government stimulus package.

People with jobs buy things. So the communities that have been suffering from the closing of mines and wells would once again thrive.

And the good news doesn't stop there.   As energy becomes abundant and affordable, the cost of products that are produced or delivered with energy, which is every product, goes down. That helps to control rising inflation, making everyone's wages worth more, not less.

It also affects our trade deficit. One third of America's trade deficit comes from our importation of energy. In the global marketplace, we should be the energy producers of the world, not the energy consumers. There is a real marketplace for energy out there, and we have lost out on the benefits because we haven't entered the arena. Freeing America's energy gets us into the game, with a winning economic team.

That brings us to the Middle East. If America were not only energy independent, but a global energy supplier, the terrorists who fund their operations with oil dollars would find themselves without the resources they need to continue buying arms and equipment or running their training camps. We would not just stop being a customer to people who use American oil dollars to buy guns to shoot at Americans, we would be competing in the world energy marketplace for all their other customers as well. The best way to fight terrorism is to bankrupt the terrorists. And a vibrant American energy industry can be a large part of that effort.

The final good is the effect on the American dollar. If we were supplying energy, we could insist that our international customers pay in American dollars. Keeping the dollar in use as the international energy currency helps to protect us from runaway inflation, buying us time to deal with some of the other areas where Washington has gotten it wrong.

In real life, removing Washington's tentacles in one area can stop the strangulation in many. Let's give America a Washington tentacle-ectomy.

Limits

Isn't it interesting that even though every political expert repeatedly informs us that this election is all about the economy, the candidates and their super PAC's run commercials that attack the pro-life credentials of their opponents? If abortion doesn't matter, why does it keep coming up?

Because the societal effects of abortion reach far beyond the single issue.

In the candidate discussions, we have been hearing a great deal about how Roe v Wade was an improper decision because the Supreme Court overstepped its bounds. It did, but that is not why abortion is wrong.

It would still be wrong if it had been passed by Congress and signed into law by the President.
The manner of legalization is irrelevant. It is the thing that was legalized that matters here.

In the legalization of abortion the government declared that it had the ability to decide who had a right to his own life. That legalization moved life from the category of unalienable right to privilege. It made the existence of every person subject to the whim of the state.

If our very right to exist needs government approval, we should not be surprised when that same government is now deciding that it can impose limits and conditions on liberty or property ownership or personal opportunity. We should not be surprised when the same folks who defend this power of the state do not feel that they are bound by any of the rules that apply to the rest of us. And we should not be surprised when the areas where government must grant approval for our existence begin to expand.

In the final analysis, abortion is not an issue – it is a line. A line that says there are areas beyond the control of the state. The right of each of us to exist is outside of that line.

In the ads currently running about abortion, some of the candidates are accusing others of allowing funding for "some abortions". And while the ads making those accusations are, to say the least, misleading in their presentations, the underlying fact reveals that many of the initiatives undertaken in the name of defending the lives of unborn children have allowed for exceptions to the protections being sought.

At one level, the use of the word "exceptions" is a travesty. In a delivery room, no "exceptions" have ever appeared. There are only ever little boys or little girls. And no matter what difficulties surrounded the conceptions or gestations of those children – they are STILL children.

At a deeper level, the ads themselves point out the fact that the laws passed in those efforts were just as much on the wrong side of the line limiting the power of the government as Roe v Wade itself. It does not matter if the government declares that one person, one thousand persons, or one million persons can only exist with government approval – it's the "exist with government approval" that is the problem.

If the government can say that any of us need its approval to exist, it has actually said that about all of us. And if our very right to our own existences has been stripped away, then we truly are just the property of an almighty State.

Fighting to protect the unalienable right of unborn boys and girls to exist is actually fighting to preserve the fundamental principle of our American heritage – that we are endowed by a Creator with rights that are beyond the reach of any government.

Climbing the Ladder

In the debate over illegal immigration, perhaps it we should begin with the words of the Emma Lazarus poem inscribed on the base of the Statue of Liberty:

Give me your tired, your poor,
Your huddled masses, yearning to breathe free, ...

It's interesting that America did not ask for the rich and famous, she welcomed those who had nothing. And they came by the thousands. In fact, almost all of us can identify at least one ancestor who passed by that inscription.

The question that needs to be asked in today's debate is, "Why did they come?"

The short answer is that in America they didn't HAVE TO be a member of the huddled masses.

If they followed the rules and worked hard, they had a chance to climb out of the huddle. It was as if America suspended a ladder over the head of every person who passed that Statue, and offered that person the challenge of climbing it. And while a guarantee of success is never possible, there was a guarantee of opportunity for those willing to accept America's challenge.

It didn't matter what country you came from because now you were an American. And our ancestors were proud to proclaim themselves as such. They embraced the culture, the language, and the opportunity, and built a place that continues to attract those who want something more for themselves and their children.

Illegal immigration attacks every aspect of that reality.

The attack begins with undermining the very foundation of the liberty that sustains our greatness – equality before the law.

Illegal immigration says that only some people have to follow the rules, that behavior has only has consequences some of the time. And when those who try to follow the rules see that the ones who break them are not only allowed to do so, but actually receive benefits from their noncompliance, the ranks of the non-compliant grow.

The second attack is on the illegal immigrants themselves. Most of them came for the same reasons as the people who passed by our Statue. They were looking for something more.

The responsibility for enforcing America's rules does not belong to them. It belongs to every elected official who decided to ignore his obligation to enforce the laws of this nation. It belongs to every employer who decided that hiring an illegal under the table was cheaper than hiring an American above it. It belongs to every special interest group that decided that it could build its ranks, and therefore its influence, on the backs of the immigrants.

Our immigrant ancestors, who followed the rules, either learned English themselves, or made sure their children did, as quickly as possible. So they did not require an organization of translators to participate in American life. They got legitimate jobs, where they not only paid taxes, but they could be promoted. So they did not require the assistance of any government agency. They not only voted, they could run for office. So they could become full participants in not just our culture, but our government.

For the most part, illegal immigrants don't learn to speak English, they don't get legitimate jobs, and they can't run for office. The ladder of opportunity that comes with entering America correctly is never offered to them.

Instead, America now has a sub-culture that is not American existing within its borders.

And the combination of rewarding rule-breaking and enabling a non-American culture creates a progression that eventually moves a society from liberty-based-on-law to anarchy-based-on-fear to tyranny-based-on-power.

When the progression is completed, America will no longer need to worry about illegal immigration.

Changing the Question

There is an exercise that is often presented to students called the "Lifeboat". In the exercise, there is a lifeboat with ten people in it. The students are given a bio of each of the people, and then told that only nine will fit in the boat. They are instructed to decide who must be tossed out of the boat so the remaining nine people will survive.

Over the years, students have struggled with the task of deciding who should live and who should die. As the exercise proceeds, the class then discusses the decision of each student. No student is comfortable with the task, but most do not know how to escape the horrible decision-making process the exercise requires.

But one time, a student came into class with a different answer. This student offered the possibility of using clothing to make a rope, and then letting each passenger swim behind the boat for a one hour shift. With this approach, there are never more than nine people in the boat at one time, and no one has to die.

The class listened to this new solution, and suddenly they had a variety of other options that would allow all ten passengers to survive. The professor asked why the new options had not been offered first, and the students replied that no one had asked them to come up with solutions that would save every life. They had been asked to choose a life to end, and they had focused on answering the question that had been asked.

The student with the new approach had changed the question. Instead of asking which life to end, that student had asked himself how to save every life. When the question changed, the answer did as well.

Today, the federal government looks at every situation by asking, "How can Washington deal with this"? When that is the question, the answer will always revolve around a federal program or policy.   No one stops to even consider any other alternative because human minds tend to focus on the question that has been asked.

The Washington establishment works hard to make that sure that no one stops to think about the fact that they are controlling the underlying question. Everything is a crisis that must be immediately solved, so no one is given time to thoroughly evaluate any situation.

But what if we took the time? What if we changed the question? What if we asked, "Should Washington be dealing with this" instead of just assuming that only Washington has the answers we seek?

All of sudden, things would look very different. Washington involvement would not be a given, it would just be one option among many. The federal government would have to prove that it was the best equipped entity to solve the particular problem being investigated. And in many cases, it would not be considered the most effective option.

If we truly want to change the direction that America has been taking in the past decades, we need to begin by following the example of the student in that classroom. We need to change the questions that we ask.

Imagine the new and incredible solutions we could find if we did.

Created for Freedom

Stand in front of a mirror and ask the person you see this question:

"When your government looks at you, do you want it to see a creature of an all powerful State, or do you want it to see a creation of an almighty and eternal Father to whom both you and the officials of that government will be accountable someday?"

Two hundred and thirty-six years ago, a group of Americans asked themselves that same question. Their answer became the foundation of a new country, and was recorded in the document we know as the Declaration of Independence.

They were creations, with both the rights and the responsibilities of that status. And in order to protect their rights so they could honor their responsibilities, they were required to stand against a government that refused to recognize that truth.

Afterwards, they formed a government that they hoped would continue to recognize each citizen as a creation. They knew that this required strong fences to limit the might of the government, and they wrote a Constitution that included those fences.

But in the final analysis, protecting our rights and honoring our responsibilities as creations lies in our hands. No document can magically limit the power of the government unless we insist that the government obey its provisions.

We have not done so.

For example, the Constitution explicitly says that Congress has the power to tax income. It does not say that Congress has the power to use taxes to control the behavior of citizens. It does not say that Congress does NOT have the power to use taxes to control the behavior of citizens. It does not address that issue at all.

But we the citizens addressed that issue long ago, and we said it was okay with us. We have allowed our taxes to be adjusted if we bought a home, or added weatherization, or paid student loan interest, or placed money in IRA accounts, or … And not only have we passively given permission, many of us have actively worked to add things to the list of tax "breaks".

But a tax break for one person is a tax punishment for another. If person A buys weatherization and person B buys new bedroom furniture, but only person A gets the tax break, aren't we actually punishing person B for not buying weatherization?

The issue is not really weatherization, or even health care.

The issue is whether or not the government has the power to use taxes to control the behavior of its citizens, effectively making those citizens the property of the state.
Will we allow ourselves to become nothing more than creatures of an all powerful state, who can be "molded" through economic and legal carrots and sticks into compliance, or will we retain our status as creations of that almighty and eternal Father?

On this national birthday, we would do well to remember that we can only exercise our endowed rights by honoring our endowed responsibilities. And protecting and preserving the freedom that each of us was created for is the most fundamental of those responsibilities.

As You Reap

The latest FBI report over the scandal at Penn State has resulted in the predictable level of finger pointing, and Monday morning quarterbacking. The general consensus is that the abuse was allowed to continue because protecting the prestige and income of the university's football program was considered to be more important than protecting the well-being of innocent, but invisible, children.

Everyone is outraged that this was the case. The experts agree that the lives and well-being of innocent children should never have been put at risk for any economic or reputational reason.

The problem is that Penn State did not exist in a vacuum. Its culture is a microcosm of what is happening in America today.

Because in America today, protecting the lives of the innocent, but invisible, children who die every day in abortion mills across this country is just not a top priority. The same experts who are loudly decrying what occurred at Penn State tell us that we need to put these tiny children "on the back burner" until we protect our national economic and reputational interests.

And how, exactly, is this different from the decision-making matrix used by the officials at Penn State?

The reality is that it is not different. It is just as wrong, and innocent children are dying because of our indifference.

No one is saying that economics is not important. But this is NOT a nation that was founded on a dollar sign. It is a nation that was founded on Truth.

The most fundamental truth is that each of us is a unique and priceless creation of an eternal Father, and as such, has unalienable rights. The instant that we abandon that truth, we lose everything that America was intended to be.

And no amount of wealth can ever replace it.

Penn State is a tragedy, and an opportunity. We can either open our eyes to the culture that allowed those children to be harmed, or we can hide behind finger-pointing. We can resolve to put protecting self-evident truth above protecting dollar bills, or we can try to convince ourselves that it was just about a football program so we don't have to deal with the larger, and more uncomfortable, issues.

The victims at Penn State eventually became visible to all of us. The victims of abortion will largely remain anonymous.

But our indifference to their suffering will, in the end, prove to be just as devastating to the future of this nation as the current scandal is to the university that allowed it to occur.

Co-exist?

We have all seen the bumper stickers that say, "Coexist" with the letters stylized to represent the various religions around the world. On the surface, the sentiment is lovely.

The difficulty arises when one looks a bit deeper. If there truly is a desire to peaceably co-exist, then we should be seeing evidence of commitment to that desire coming from every religion symbolized in the slogan.

But we aren't.

The May 2012 edition of FrontPageMag.com includes the following excerpts from a report on Christian persecution in Muslim nations in the month of April.

In Nigeria, a church was bombed during Easter Sunday, killing some 50 worshippers.

In Turkey, a pastor was beaten by Muslims immediately following Easter service and threatened with death unless he converts to Islam.

In Kenya, Muslims threw grenades into an open-air Christian church gathering, killing a woman and a boy, and wounding 50. In a separate incident, a Muslim man pretending to be a worshipper at a church threw three grenades during the service, killing a 27-year-old university student and injuring 16.

In the Sudan, a Christian compound in Khartoum was stormed by a throng of Muslims "armed with clubs, iron rods, a bulldozer and fire," the day after a Muslim leader called on Muslims to destroy "the infidels' church." "Police at the compound stood back and did nothing to prevent the mob from vandalizing the compound."

In Tunisia, after the Russian ambassador in Tunis specifically requested the nation's Ministry of Interior to "protect the Orthodox church," both the Russian school located behind the church and the Christian cemetery were vandalized. The walls of the school and religious frescoes were smeared with fecal matter, while the cemetery's crosses were destroyed.

In Algeria, a Christian was sentenced to five years in prison for "shaking the faith" of Muslims.

In Bangladesh, a former Muslim prayer leader who converted to Christianity was beaten almost to death by members of his Muslim community, causing him to be hospitalized for almost two months.

In Egypt, a juvenile court sentenced a Coptic Christian teenager to three years in prison for allegedly "insulting Islam." Another judge upheld a six-year prison sentence for a Christian convicted of "blasphemy" for "insulting the prophet."

In Iran, a Christian convert from Islam has been sentenced to six years in prison.

In Pakistan, a Christian man was arrested and charged with "blasphemy" for rescuing his 8-year-old nephew from a beating at the hands of Muslim boys who sought to force the boy to convert to Islam.

In the Philippines, a former Muslim who became a Christian pastor was murdered in front of his wife in his home. Another pastor was shot in the head five times and killed by two "unknown gunmen" in front of his teenage daughter.

In India, Muslims stormed a home where a Christian prayer meeting was being held, beating the Christians, including a 65-year-old widow. The Muslims "called them pagans as they kicked, slapped and pushed the Christians…. one Muslim, "brandishing a sickle, chased many of them, hurling all kinds of insults and attempting to murder them all…. 500 Muslims had gathered and were watching in amusement as the extremists chased and harassed the Christians for about 90 minutes."

Keep in mind that all of the above, and more, happened *in the single month* of April. The list is just as long in every other month. There are no similar reports about any other religion. Just Islam.

So, if the Islamic community is actually serious about co-existing with the rest of us, perhaps they should start inside their own house.   Until and unless they do, their rhetoric about co-existing is at best hypocritical and at worst dangerous. And we would be wise to remember that reality.

Words Matter

A stand-up comedian once did an act that talked about how important it is to use the correct words when we speak. He gave a few examples to illustrate his point. The most dramatic involved the synonymous phrases, "I'm sorry," and "I apologize", if spoken at a funeral.

He was being funny, but mis-used words are hurting America.

Let's start with the word, "family". The definition of family is a group of people who are related by blood, marriage, or adoption. The definition is as old as humanity. Yet we now are told that our schools are families, our churches are families, and our businesses are families. The obvious question is how these folks are related by blood, marriage or adoption, and the obvious answer is that they are not.

By calling every group a family, we dilute the actual meaning of the word. That means that real families, the ones related by blood or marriage or adoption, are no longer considered unique and special.

So at a time when we most need the permanence and stability of the traditional family in America, we have effectively redefined the word, and therefore the institution, to mean any group of people who have come together for some purpose and who can enter or exit the group at any time.

The next word is "community". This one is not used enough.

Community is the group of people who come together with a common purpose. We can join a community if we embrace the purpose, no matter where we came from. Our schools and churches and businesses are communities.

So is America. This nation is, or was created to be, a community of people who shared a heritage and a future. The heritage began with the understanding that each of us is endowed with rights by a Creator beyond the government and therefore was to be accorded the opportunity to achieve. The future grew from that understanding, as each member of the American community acted on the opportunity in our heritage, and worked to achieve his dreams.

When we lost the word community, we lost the shared purpose that the word embodied. And now we are watching America disintegrate into ever-smaller sets of disparate groups, all fighting with each other over perceived inequities or insults.

This situation brings us to the last word, "discrimination". It means the unjust treatment of someone. Period.

But today, it is only "discrimination" if certain groups or individuals are on the receiving end of the behavior. And the government is the arbiter of the decision.

Two true examples illustrate the point.

A conservative government official took his wife and young children to a restaurant for dinner. He was sitting quietly at the table with his family when the owner of the restaurant, who did not agree with the official's politics, loudly and publicly insisted that the family leave the establishment. The owner declared that the establishment was his property, and he had the right to decide who could use his services.

A woman tried to hire a professional photographer for her lesbian wedding ceremony in a state where same-sex marriage is illegal. The photographer declined, saying that providing such a service would conflict with the religious beliefs of the owners of the company, and the owners had the right to decide who could use their services.

In both cases, property owners asserted that they had the right to direct how their property was to be used. Yet one case was determined to be discrimination and one was not, based on the beliefs of the parties involved. Now THAT is discrimination.

Family. Community. Discrimination. They are just words. And they matter.

Silent Messages

The Tony Awards were given out earlier this week. There were all the usual recognitions for best actor and actress, best director, and best writers. There was also an entire set of awards for those who work "behind the scenes" in areas such as costuming, lighting, and set design. They give those awards out before the national broadcast. The same situation exists for the annual Oscar and Emmy Awards.

The folks who work in those areas are as important as their more public counterparts in creating the messages that reach us. In fact, the message they create is often even more effective at conveying a point of view to the audience because it reaches us under our radar screens.

For example, some years ago there was a movie that retold the Cinderella story. It was called "Ever After". The movie was not only a success at the time of its release, but it is regularly seen on many of the cable stations, particularly those aimed at children. The movie has no foul language, no nudity, and no gruesome violence. It is fairly well-written, so its target audience not only enjoys it once, but will happily watch it several times. Busy parents will immediately recognize the evil stepmother and stepsisters, watch enough to see that the story is following the general lines of the fairy tale, and feel comfortable allowing their children to watch the program.

No one pays attention to the costumes.

If you did, you would notice that the evil stepmother consistently wears a large cross necklace. The particulars of the design of the necklace change with each of her costume changes, but the pendant is almost always a cross. And it is prominently displayed. At the same time, the Cinderella character NEVER wears a cross.

It is critical to remember that costume designers proactively selected every single thing that the character on the screen is wearing to help the actor or actress create a person that we will either love or hate. Most of us never consciously think about the costume, we just receive the message the costume sends us.

It's easy to say that costumes don't convey a message. Then think about Darth Vader – would he be the same without his black helmet and cape? Most of us connect black hat with bad guy, and white hat with good guy. If we consciously think about it, what possible difference can the color of a person's hat make to his character?

And that is the whole point. We don't consciously think about the connection. We just accept it.

So, in our example, the evil stepmother is associated with all things Christian, and Cinderella is not. If they both wore religious symbols in their costuming, there would be no underlying message about faith. If the stepmother wore a variety of pendants, and the cross was one among many, there would be no underlying message. But only the "bad guy" wears a cross, and she wears it all the time. The connection between things Christian and badness is unmistakable, and our children received that connection without even being aware that it was being transmitted.

The hostility of the entertainment industry to traditional values is not a secret. If we are to teach our children to recognize and resist their agenda, we need to pay as much attention to the silent messages on the screen as we do to the spoken ones.

Freedom of Worship

If you have been carefully listening, you will notice that when government officials now talk about religion and the Constitution, they refer to our guaranteed "freedom of worship" instead of "freedom of religion". It's only one word, so it is easy to miss the change; but the difference between worship and religion is enormous.

Let's put it into sports terms.

Instead of freedom to root for your favorite NFL team, you will now have the freedom to cheer for that team.

That means that while you are in the stadium of your team during a scheduled game, you may cheer your head off. But once you leave the stadium, you may not display the team name or logo in any form in your school or in your workplace. You may not wear any clothing that includes the name or logo of the team to any public event. You may not engage in discussions with others about the merits of your team. You may not invite others to join you in becoming fans of that team. And you may not compare the accomplishments of your team to those of any other team.

In effect, when you leave the stadium, you must leave your allegiance to your team behind.

Unfortunately, the situation is even worse.

The rules above only apply to the fans of SOME teams. So the fans of the Screaming Aardvarks are required to follow the rules above, while the fans of the Charging Platypuses are not only permitted to continue publicly supporting their team, they are given the ability to force Aardvark fans to participate in activities that will help the Platypuses.

Aardvark fans must attend seminars to learn about the merits of the Platypuses. They must attend at least one Platypus game each season or pay a fine. They must express their support of the Platypuses whenever asked about the topic, or face penalties. They must not, under any circumstances, do or say anything to convert anyone from supporting the Platypuses to supporting the Aardvarks.

That is freedom of worship.

You may participate in your faith inside the church building, but once you leave that building, you must leave your allegiance to your faith behind. And not only must you leave that allegiance behind, you must be willing to publicly embrace ideologies and practices that are exactly the opposite of what your faith teaches, or be penalized.

No sports fan in the country would accept such a situation. Can you imagine what would happen if the government took even one single step in that direction?

Yet that same government is working to create a situation in which those of us who live lives illuminated by faith are accorded fewer rights than the average sports enthusiast.
Freedom of worship is NOT freedom of religion. It is not even a part of freedom of religion because it requires believers to jettison their faith at the church doors.   It is a travesty of the words in our First Amendment.

If we are to preserve the America we cherish, we must become as adamant as NFL fans in telling the government that it will not be allowed to take even one single step in that direction.

Freedom's Catch 22

In a novel published in 1961, author Joseph Heller describes a pilot who tries to get himself declared insane so he won't have to fly any more combat missions. The doctor informs him that since no sane person would volunteer for such dangerous duty, the very fact that he is requesting a psychiatric evaluation proves that he is sane and therefore able to continue to fly combat missions. The doctor explains that although this would mean that the other pilots must be insane, no mental evaluation is done without a request, so they will never be evaluated and can continue to fly combat missions.

The phrase Catch 22 comes from the title of that book, and has come to mean a situation in which an individual cannot avoid a problem because of contradictory rules and regulations. The person is trapped.

We are looking at a Catch 22 in the struggle of the Catholic Church to maintain its right to religious freedom in its own institutions.

The administration's health care mandate includes language that requires all institutions to pay for contraception access in insurance plans, even if the institution is self-insured. If an organization does not wish to comply with this mandate, the option is to stop providing health care benefits to any employee, and instead pay the fines imposed on employers who do not pay such benefits. The size of the fines would result in the closing of the institutions in question.

The "exemption" granted for religious organizations stipulates that the organization must be entirely self-contained. In other words, to qualify for the exemption, the organization in question must hire and serve only members of the particular faith that the organization subscribes to.

For example, a Catholic hospital could only hire staff members who were Catholic, and could only admit patients who were Catholics.

So, what if the Catholic hospital decided to comply with the requirements to receive the exemption and only hire and admit those who are members of the Catholic faith?

The hospital would find itself in violation of the non-discrimination requirements of federal law. Those requirements explicitly specify that hiring practices must conform to equal opportunity standards, and services must be provided equally to all, without regard to things like religion.

If the hospital did not comply with these non-discrimination requirements, it would lose its eligibility for federal programs such as Medicare funding. Without access to Medicare reimbursements, the hospital would have to close.

Catch 22.

The obvious question is, are the leaders in the Obama administration unaware of the Catch 22 they have created?

This is the administration that required Georgetown University to cover religious symbols before the President appeared on campus. It is the administration that revoked conscience clause protections for health care workers in federal regulations. It is the administration that forgives student loans in exchange for community service, but ruled that service in religious organizations is ineligible. It is the administration that declared that the First Amendment does not protect churches when hiring pastors and rabbis. It is the administration that refused to comply with a U.S. Supreme Court order to transfer ownership of the land to private hands and re-erect the cross in the WWII memorial in the Mojave Desert.

It is, therefore, almost impossible to believe that this Catch 22 is inadvertent. Nor is it really about contraceptives.

It is the latest battle in the war against religious liberty being waged in this country. It is a battle, and a war, that we cannot afford to lose.

The Power of One

The news is, frankly, rotten. Corruption is everywhere. We have allowed ourselves to be divided into subsets of disconnected groups all constantly at war with each other. The fabric of our society is unraveling, with everything from constant vulgarity to unchecked violence becoming the norm instead of the exception. The list is almost endless.

It's easy to give in to the temptation to crawl into the nearest closet, lock the door behind us, and hope that Gabriel blows that trumpet soon.

It's also wrong.

This is not the first time in history that a society faced chaos.

And in those times of challenge, there were those who refused to yield. We know some of their names, and some will remain hidden from our view until the end of time. In most cases, they were not folks that the world would consider to be among the proverbial rich and famous. In fact, many of them died in less than wonderful circumstances.

We often refer to them as martyrs.

Martyr is a funny word. When we use it to speak of someone who lived in the past, it is a word that carries an air of honor and integrity. But when we use it to refer to someone who is currently alive and well, it is almost an insult. Someone is "just being a martyr."

You have to wonder if the martyrs we remember with honor heard the same insulting tone during their own lifetimes. It's a good bet that they did.

The word, which simply means witness, implies that there is one particular thing for which a person will stand in witness, no matter what the cost.

Not everyone is willing to be such a witness.

But when an individual makes the decision that there actually is something that he is willing to witness, no matter the cost, that individual becomes a force in society. The power of that one person's witness increases as the cost of that witness grows.

There is something incredibly compelling about something that a person is willing to sacrifice all he has or is to preserve his witness to it. That is why, for example, that the more the Roman Empire threw the early Christians into stadiums filled with lions, the more other Roman citizens decided that they should look into a faith that was so strong that believers would die rather that recant. In the end, the Empire itself bowed to the power of that witness.

Thankfully, for most of us, death will not be the end result of our witness. That does not diminish its necessity or its power.

So, in a world filled with corruption, we can decide NOT to be corrupt – to be the one person who is known to be completely honest and fair our dealings with others. In a world filled with anger and hatred, we can decide NOT to give in to our own negative feelings – to be the one person who is known to have a kind word for, and about, everyone around us. In a world filled with vulgarity and rudeness, we can decide NOT to be a bore – to be the one person who is known for courtesy.

It seems like such an effort would be meaningless. It's not.

It reminds those around us that there is a different, and a better, way. It gives them a vision of what America is supposed to be.

So, are we going to stay in the closet, or are we going to become witnesses to the values that made America great?

Don't Impose….

This week many of us received e-mails telling us to check our gasoline receipts because gas stations in places across the country had reset their pumps to cheat their customers. The pumps would register and charge for more gasoline than was actually pumped, and the station owner would pocket the extra money.

At the same time, many of us are also seeing signs at gas stations that tell us that all cash customers must pre-pay for gasoline because they have had so many consumers fill their tanks and then just drive away without paying.

So, while consumers are asking the government to investigate and prosecute the station owners who are rigging their pumps, station owners are asking the government to investigate and prosecute consumers who are leaving without paying. In both cases, the aggrieved side is looking to have new laws passed to impose harsher penalties on the perpetrators.

We used to agree on a single law that dealt with both sides of this situation. We used to display that law on government buildings and teach it in our schools. It was a simple law.

It said, "Thou shalt not steal."

It was part of a larger code of laws that we used to agree was a necessary part of American culture. That code began by acknowledging that there was an ultimate lawgiver, who did not change, and to whom all of us were accountable. The laws in that code were not complicated. In fact, the entire code fit on two stone tablets.

As we move farther away from that code, we find that we need to create an almost endless series of rules to deal with every conceivable situation – like "Don't rig the gas pumps" and "Don't take gas from gas pumps without paying". And that ever-growing set of rules comes with a matching growth in government investigative, enforcement, and punitive agencies.

We used to just say that it was wrong to steal – no matter what the circumstances of the stealing happened to be. But since the concept of "wrong" brings us back to that original code and the original lawgiver, we cannot use that word.

We can only talk about what is legal, so our only alternative to deal with situations like our gasoline dilemma is to make the particular behavior illegal. That means that every behavior will need a law to govern it. The thousands and thousands of pages in our current legal code are just the beginning. And every new code will need new government powers to make it work.

The sad reality is that it doesn't matter how many new laws are written. As long as we let people focus on legal and illegal, they will find ways to get around the law.

And that is the basic problem in today's America.

"Thou shalt not steal" was a moral concept, not a legal one. It was based on the notion that the legality of an action was not as important as it righteousness. So even if there was no specific law dealing with rigging a gas pump or driving away without paying, it was still wrong and therefore unacceptable.

We are told that clinging to that original code is bad, that we do not have the right to impose our morality on others.

But perhaps a little moral imposition is just what America needs.

What's Right with America

We have all heard so much bad news that I thought it would be nice to remember what makes this nation worth fighting for.

Last night my high school senior son was driving to Pittsburgh. It was raining, and he lost control of the car on the slick, wet highway.

Thankfully, he was not injured, but since he had plowed through a highway sign, he had two flat tires with bent wheel rims, making the car un-drivable. He was an hour away from home, on a wooded section of a four lane highway, at twilight.

It was still raining.

As I drove to collect him, his brother began searching for service station options near the accident site so we wouldn't have to tow the car all the way home. It was difficult since no one knew the exact location of the accident, and we had no landmarks to work with.

He had no suggestions to give me at the time of my arrival.

I pulled up in front of the car, and my son got out. We were just beginning to discuss options when a car pulled up behind us and a young man got out. He had stopped to help. He didn't know about cars, but he was from the area, and he provided the name and location of a tire store that, it turned out, was less than 3 miles away from our location.

The tow was the next hurdle. I have a towing service attached to my phone. I called them and was trying to describe the location so they could arrange for a pickup. They wanted some kind of "anchor" landmark to give the towing company.

There was a business a bit more than half a mile farther down the road, and although it was closed, they had a sign out. We drove down the shoulder until we could see the name so I could give it to the towing people. Then I slowly backed up down the same shoulder until I was back in front of the damaged vehicle.

As I was on the phone, another gentleman stopped. When he got out of his car, I could see that he was a mechanic who was obviously going home after working late. He examined the car, and asked if there was a spare tire.

Then he suggested that he could use the spare to replace one of the damaged tires. That still left the other one.

He removed the second tire, and manually hammered the rim back into shape. Then he returned to his company's shop and came back with an air compressor to refill the tire. He had to make two trips to get all the parts he needed.

He did all of this in the rain.
As a result of his help, we were able to drive the car the few miles to the tire shop instead of having to get a tow.

Then he refused all offers of payment, telling me that he had six kids of his own, and he would want someone to help them if they were stuck. So we shook hands, and he got back into his truck and went home.

We all know that there is much that is wrong in America.

That man, and all the men and women like him, remind us that there is also much that is still right in America as well.

Tell the Truth

This weekend, the nation will honor its men and women in uniform. There will be parades and dinners and memorial services in nearly every town in America. Government officials will make speeches about how we honor those who have served, and those who serve today.

Sadly, for too many of those officials, the speeches are just plain lies.

If those in Washing truly honored the men and women who defend us with their lives, they would stop hiding the truth about what happened at places like Little Rock and Fort Hood. The fact is that the military personnel who were killed and injured were the victims of self-professed jihadists.

In Little Rock, one soldier was killed and one was injured in a drive-by shooting on a military recruiting office. Muslim convert Abdulhakim Mujahid Muhammad told police that he had intended to kill as many American Army personnel as possible. He stated that he had been sent by al-Qaeda, and that "the attack was justified according to Islamic Laws and the Islamic religion." He was allowed to plead guilty, which avoided a public trial.

At Fort Hood, the gun man, Nidal Malik Hasan, reportedly shouted, "Allahu Akbar!" (God is greatest) immediately before killing 13 people and wounding 29 others. Although Hasan was a major in the U.S. Army, his business cards did not mention his military position or rank, stating instead that he was a psychiatrist and including the title "SoA". "SoA" is the acronym for "Soldier of Allah" commonly found on jihadist websites. After the shooting, al-Qaeda spokesman Adam Gadahm praised the attack, called Hasan a "pioneer, a trailblazer and a role model."

The House of Representatives has included a provision in its recently passed National Defense Authorization Act to award Purple Hearts to the military victims of these attacks. The

Obama administration is threatening to veto the bill unless it is stripped of this provision.

The fact that this provision is necessary is, in itself, a slap at our military. The Department of Defense has the authority to declare combat status in order to award Purple Hearts, and used that authority for the Pentagon victims of the September 11 attacks. They have refused to do so for the victims of Little Rock and Fort Hood, instead issuing a statement that they were examining "the threat of violent Islamist extremism in the context of a broader threat of workplace violence."

It takes less than two minutes on the Internet to discover that our military are considered prime targets for terrorism, no matter where they are. For example, Hasan's imam, al-Awlaki openly praised the Fort Hood massacre, saying, "Nidal opened fire on soldiers who were on their way to be deployed to Iraq and Afghanistan. How can there be any dispute about the virtue of what he has done? "

That is NOT random workplace violence. Unless the members of this administration are illiterate, they are knowingly advancing their political agenda at the expense of the safety of our troops.

So our military not only has to watch for those who shoot them from the front, they have to guard against a Commander-in-Chief who allows them to be shot in the back, and then works to cover up the truth behind each attack.

If we truly want to honor our military, let's skip the parades, and demand that the truth behind incidents like Little Rock and Fort Hood be acknowledged and acted upon.

Why Celebrate?

This is America's time on the calendar. Memorial Day is barely behind us, and within the next six weeks, we will be celebrating Flag Day and the Fourth of July. That we Americans think this nation of ours is worth joyful recognition is obvious. What is not so obvious to many is why.

Perhaps two brief stories will help. Both of them happened to me.

The first occurred when I was still in high school. I spent a summer studying in Europe. We stayed mostly in France, but once in a while we took a bus to shop in Germany. My German was, to be kind, awful; but I was the only one who spoke German at all, so I usually went along as interpreter.

On this day, I asked a sales clerk the price of an object for a friend. At least, I thought that I asked the price. But when she looked at me with a blank expression, I knew that I had said something nonsensical. So, since we were only a few miles from the French border, and I thought that people probably crossed the line to shop regularly, I switched to French.

It was like waving the proverbial red flag in front of a bull. She became irate. I got so flustered that I switched to English to ask what was wrong. She immediately calmed down, smiled, and asked if I was a Yank.

It was like watching the words in the history books about the centuries-old hatred between the French and the Germans come alive right in front of me.

The second incident happened during the Bosnian/Croatian war. I was helping someone who was trying to bring the babies abandoned in that torn country across the ocean to be adopted in America. The Bosnians and the Croats would not even speak with each other to work out a way to facilitate the process.

So a friend and I went to New York to meet with the American representative of the Patriarch of that region. He told us to forget about trying to work with the warring parties over there because there was no way for us to break through hatreds that were centuries old. He counseled us to meet with Americans of Bosnian descent and Americans of Croatian descent, work out the details, and then present them as a done deal to the folks we were negotiating with.

We asked him if we would have any luck with the American side. I will never forget his answer.

He said that in America, people leave old hatreds and stereotypes behind. They become part of the American community, and their membership in that community enables them to build bridges instead of walls.

I remembered my experience in the store in Germany, and realized that I had already seen what the community of America could do. In America, there is no hatred between French and German.

It is often referred to as the American melting pot. The people who came here added to the richness of our culture by joining the community we call America. It is a community that is not based on your past, but on your future. It is a community free from the hatreds that plague so much of our world.

There is not another like it anywhere on the planet. It is not just unique, but exceptional. We who have the privilege to live in it are truly blessed.

It is, therefore, only proper for us to recognize and celebrate that blessing.

Dear Mr. President,

When I first heard about your interview with Jessica Yellin on CNN, I thought I misunderstood what you said. So I checked.

You really did say that you hadn't done enough to develop relationships with members of Congress so you could do your job properly because you wanted to be home at 6:30 in the evenings to have dinner with your daughters and help them with their homework.

So would every other mom and dad in America.

But we can't just choose not to do our jobs properly so we can fulfill that wish, unless we want to either lose our jobs, or lose our homes.

Perhaps you just don't understand what life is like for middle-class Americans, and how your failure to do your job has made that life more difficult.

Let me give you just one example.

When you began your administration, the average price of a gallon of gasoline was $1.78. Today it is $3.82. It now costs each of us an extra $24.00 every time we fill a 12 gallon tank. A parent who is making minimum wage has to spend 3 extra hours at work to earn enough to cover the difference, and he has to spend that much extra time for every single fill-up. That parent would like to be having dinner with his kids every night.

The effect of higher gas prices doesn't end at the pump. Every product that is made or delivered using gasoline is affected. That includes things like office supplies and equipment. Businesses with salaried, professional employees are seeing their profits eaten away by the increasing costs. They respond by telling those employees that they have to work longer hours for the same pay so the company can stay in business.

Those parents aren't working longer hours to increase their earnings, they are working longer hours just to keep their jobs. And they, too, would like to be having dinner with their kids every night.

For many Americans, the job disappeared despite their efforts. When companies like General Motors moved manufacturing plants from America to China, thousands of American moms and dads had to find other work. Many of them needed to take two, or even three, lower-paying jobs to replace their incomes since the mortgage didn't change when the employment did. They would also like to be having dinner with their kids every night.

Perhaps the problem is that you didn't understand what the job of the President really entailed. But Mr. President, you asked for that job, and you promised us that you would fulfill its requirements.

Now, you are telling us that you chose not to do that. In your interview, you said that you hoped that your daughters would need less of your time in the next four years so maybe you could actually honor your commitment to the American people, and spend enough time at your job to get things done.

I am sorry, Mr. President, but that is just not good enough.

We all have children too. We all love our children just as much as you love yours. You do not have the right to expect all of us to work many extra hours because you have decided that you should not have to work ANY extra hours.

And frankly, Mr. President, it is insulting to ask us to allow you to continue to do so.

Very respectfully,

An American Mom

While America Slept

In the 1930's, two powerful leaders played international chess. The fate of the entire world would be determined by the outcome of the game. The first leader wanted peace, so he continued to allow his opponent to advance without active opposition. He believed that "no one really wants war", so if he just avoided confrontation, the situation would resolve itself. He justified the harm his actions caused to those who were caught, and then harmed, in his opponent's advances by telling himself and others that he was avoiding the ultimate conflict.

As it turned out, he was wrong. He completely failed to understand that his opponent wanted world domination, and if war were part of the cost of achieving that goal, then war was an acceptable option. So his opponent took full advantage of every backward step, and used each of them to strengthen his forces for the day when war would come. And when the opponent believed that there was sufficient strength in those forces, he began that war himself.

The first leader not only failed to avoid war, he gave his opponent the time to create the war under the most unfavorable circumstances possible for his own nation, and, as it turned out, the entire world.

Both men went down in history. The first leader was Neville Chamberlain of England, and the second was Adolf Hitler of Germany.

Today there are also two powerful forces playing international chess with the fate of the entire world hanging in the balance. The first force is centered in America, and the second is centered in Islam.

The American leadership is following the same course as Mr. Chamberlain. They continue to assure everyone that "no one really wants war", so if we just avoid confrontation the situation will resolve itself. And they look the other way to avoid seeing the harm being done to those who have come under the domination of Islam.

Their judgment is as wrong as Mr. Chamberlain's was.

Islam wants world domination, and if war is part of the cost of achieving that goal, then war is not only an acceptable option – it is the preferred option. Islamic leaders take full advantage of every backward step America takes, using each as an opportunity to strengthen Islam.

The latest attacks in Egypt and Libya are a sadly perfect example of this reality.

Attacking an American embassy and killing an American ambassador is an act of war. American soil was invaded and American non-combatant lives were lost.

Our response?

We apologized for some private citizen who made a movie that offended the sensibilities of Moslems. We are passing a federal spending bill that continues to give American money to both Libya and Egypt. We are silently watching as the President of Egypt calls for the prosecution of the American citizen who made the movie, as if hurt feelings over a film justified the violence and the murders.

The Islamic community is watching, and gauging our response. And they are happily using our oil money, and our foreign aid, to continue strengthening themselves for the confrontation that lies ahead.

A confrontation that they not only welcome, but seek.

We would be wise to wake up to that truth. Or in future years, history will record that the fate of the world was decided while America slept.

All The Wrong Places

The news these days is enough to make any sane person start looking for a closet to hide in.

Children were shot in a school in a small Cleveland suburb – by a child. Two of the victims have died.

A group of ethicists in Australia has published an article in a journal of medical ethics arguing that we allow "after-birth-abortions", but not call them infanticides because we shouldn't think of these entities as children.

The administration has decided that cutting the health care benefits of our active-duty military (present and retired) is an acceptable way to curb spending. They have also decided that no unionized bureaucrats should be affected by this cut.

The list could continue, but we all get the point. Something is radically wrong with our society.

The question is, what should we do about it?

Many are looking to Washington for answers. The thinking is that if we just elect the right people, THEY will somehow deal with the situation.

There are two problems with this response.

The first is obvious – how do we know without doubt which people are the right people? We have elected lots of folks that we thought were the right people, only to be sadly disappointed when they got into office and joined the very establishment they promised to reform.

The second flows from the first. The ability of the establishment to corrupt an individual is enormous. Whether it is the compromises that a candidate makes to get the funds necessary to get elected, or the deals the officeholder makes in one area to get action in another, or the vote-bargaining that occurs because constituents demand their "piece of the pie", a single individual finds it nearly impossible to avoid the swamp that government has become.

Conversely, the ability of one individual to change the establishment is miniscule. Legislation that would create real reform doesn't move out of committee, or is amended so drastically that the final version is unrecognizable.

So if the answer isn't in Washington, where is it?

It's in church.

Church is the entity that reminds us that truth doesn't move, that holding power isn't the goal of existence, and that each of us is simultaneously endowed with rights and accountable for how we exercise them.

In the current conflict between the church and the state, the government is not only telling the church that it may not obey the dictates of conscience in its own institutions, it is asserting that the state may dictate what the conscience of the church should say. The particular issue doesn't matter – the state's attempt to tell a church what it may believe is the problem.

At the very moment when we most need the voice of the church, the state is working desperately to silence that voice. And if the state believes that silencing the church is a priority, we should pay attention.

When fighting an opponent, the thing that our opponent most wants is the very thing that we should strive the hardest to deny him.

In this case, that means not only preserving the voice of the church, but listening to what it has to say.

Worthless

Did you ever feel like life was a race that you couldn't win? That no matter what you did, you would never be good enough to get the prize?

First, there is our national preoccupation with physical appearance. We are not supposed to show any signs of the aging process, and we are bombarded with products and procedures that are all guaranteed to keep us looking young and beautiful. But none of them ever really make us look like we are 25 again. And most of us were never drop dead gorgeous to begin with. So every time we look in our mirrors, we are reminded that we do not quite meet the standard.

We are also supposed to be slender and fit. There are uncountable numbers of televised exercise classes and DVD's, in which all of the people exercising have nearly perfect bodies and are gracefully doing the exercise routine without actually breaking into a full sweat. And as we look down at our own perspiring and flabby limbs while we struggle to complete even the simplest workout routine, we feel that somehow we aren't good enough here either.

Then, since we are all supposed to be young and beautiful and slender and fit, we should have an equally fascinating lifestyle, with lovely houses, new cars, great jobs, and more-than-adequate income. Of course, most of us struggle with those things as well, wondering why we can't seem to keep up with the proverbial Joneses.

Finally, we enter into the area of relationships, in which each of us is absolutely certain that if the other person REALLY knew us, they would run in the other direction. So we try to hide our own failings and pretend to be "worthy". And we often accept or excuse behaviors from others because we feel that we aren't good enough for anything more, which makes us feel even more unworthy of actually being loved and valued.

But what if there was someone who already knew that we could never be "whatever" enough and didn't care? Someone who didn't bring a measuring stick into the relationship, but accepted us just as we were.

Someone who simply loved us.

This week, we celebrate the knowledge that such a person exists. He knows that we are not worthy of His love, and He loves us anyway. He understands, better than any other person, how far away from good enough each of us will always be, and He embraces us in spite of it.

We hung Him on a cross, and He forgave us, even as we were hurting Him. There was no measuring stick used there either.

He offers us a different path. A path on which we can admit that we are, in fact, worthless.

Once we admit that to ourselves, we can get off the treadmill of trying to meet the "whatever enough" standard.   Then we are free to return His embrace.

And when we do, we find out that in His eyes, we are priceless.

Happy Easter!

A Different Perspective

Today's America seems to be dominated by the word "me". There is a continual barrage of complaints from those who aren't getting everything they think they deserve. At the same time, there is a never-ending list of stories about folks who feel no remorse about cheating others to benefit themselves.

The idea of caring for and about someone other than the person we see in the mirror seems to be rapidly disappearing from our culture.

And many of us, who are trying to hold on to the ideals of honesty and fairness and compassion, too often feel like we are fighting a losing battle. The temptation to just give up can be overwhelming.

We are not the first people in history to face such temptations. So perhaps remembering the life of one who did not give in will give us the inspiration to continue our own work.

Her name was Irena Sendler. She was born in 1910, in Poland. She was a social worker when the Nazis invaded Poland.

When the Jews were rounded up into the Warsaw Ghetto, Irena joined the Polish underground sponsored movement, Zegota (Council to Aid the Jews), and became the head of its division on children.

She obtained a pass from the Nazi Epidemic Control Department so she could enter the Ghetto.

Seeing the starvation conditions and knowing that death was the final outcome for Ghetto residents, she began smuggling the children out. She hid them in toolboxes, potato sacks, gunny sacks, even coffins.

The church was an active assistant. One church had two doors, one on the Ghetto side and the other on the "Aryan" side. The children entered the church as Jews and exited as Christians, with false documents. Sendler reported that she sent most of the children to religious establishments because she knew that she could count on the sisters.

The children were given false identities and placed in adoptive homes, orphanages, and convents. Irena later stated that no one had ever refused to take a child from her. Even though, in Poland, anyone found aiding a Jew would be executed with his entire family.

Irena noted the children's original names and their new identities, and buried the records in jars beneath an apple tree in a neighbor's back yard, across the street from German barracks. She hoped that she could someday dig up the jars, locate the children and inform them of their past.

In all, the jars contained the names of 2,500 children.
In 1943 Irena was arrested, imprisoned and tortured by the Gestapo, who broke her feet and legs.

In spite of the torture, Irena did not betray the identities of any of the adoptive families, her associates, or the Jewish children.

She was sentenced to death, but escaped and lived in hiding for the rest of the war.

After the war she dug up the jars and tried to reunite the children she had placed with their natural relatives. Sadly, most of the Jewish families had perished during the Holocaust.

Irena's story was unnoticed until the year 2000, when four high school students in Kansas wrote about her as part of a history project.

She did not think of herself as a hero. The 2,500 children she saved and the generations that will follow them would disagree.

And as for us, how can we read of a story like Irena's and even THINK about quitting?

Stop the Algae!

I have listened with great interest to the debate surrounding the energy situation. If I understand the concerns of the environmentalists correctly, they are looking for an energy source that is completely renewable, does not affect the natural habitats of any place on earth, and is available to everyone equally.

Well, I am taking this opportunity to announce that I have solved the energy crisis.

All we need to do is capture the energy that comes from hot flashes.

It is completely renewable. There will always be women who are having them. In fact, nothing needs to be done to ensure that this situation continues indefinitely. We never need to worry about running out of women having hot flashes.

It does not affect the natural habitat of any place on earth. They do not need anyone to drill for them, or pump for them, or grow them. They naturally exist in an openly available form. And, other than the woman experiencing the flash, they have not been known to affect the environment in the area where the hot flash is occurring.

They are available to everyone. If there is a place where energy is needed for human endeavors, it is a sure bet that there are already women present. And since women naturally produce this energy form for several years, it should not require any government activity to ensure that the energy is available everywhere.

It does not have any of the complications of solar energy or wind energy. Solar energy needs the sun, so cloudy days and all nights are a problem. Wind energy needs the wind to actually blow with enough strength to make the wind turbines turn, so calm days are a problem. But hot flashes naturally occur at all hours of

the day and night, and they don't require any wind conditions.
They are always available as an energy source, especially with so
many women producing them.

Now, there are a few technical issues to work through.

We will need to develop a mechanism to capture this wonderful
energy source, convert it into electricity, and share it through our
power grids. And we will, of course, need to decide how to
compensate all the women who will be sharing this energy
"resource" with the rest of us.

But I am not expecting that any of these situations will prove to
be an unsolvable problem.

After all, the federal government has invested hundreds of
millions into algae and solar power and wind energy companies.
Most of them have not moved beyond the research and
development stages, and many have gone bankrupt because they
couldn't bring a viable product into the market place at an
affordable price.

So we just need the government agencies involved to divert the
funds they are already spending away from these failed
experiments and put them toward the development of the energy
source of tomorrow.

Given the enthusiasm that Washington has shown for algae, I'm
sure they will jump at this new, and better, opportunity.

Getting Sober

Anyone who has ever known a recovering alcoholic has probably heard the story of what finally caused that person to face his addiction and get sober. They also have probably heard that after the physical withdrawal symptoms have subsided, the emotional withdrawal process begins. Many recovering alcoholics find the emotional process much more arduous in the beginning, and much more freeing as they move further into sobriety.

They have to actually experience all the emotions and challenges they either deadened or escaped through the alcohol. They report that it's almost a knee-jerk reaction to say, "I can't do this!" and reach for the nearest bottle. It's only when they begin to say, "With God's help, I CAN and WILL do this!" that freedom from addiction begins.

Americans are now a nation of addicts. Only we are addicted to government. Every time a challenge or difficulty arises, we have been conditioned to turn to the government to either remove (deaden) the pain that we might feel or to help us escape the challenge that we need to conquer. And just like every other addict, we collectively deny that our dependence is a problem.

But think about so many of the conversations that we have heard or participated in about cutting government spending. The phrase, "Cut the spending but not in my program," is uttered so often that it has become a cliché.

If anyone suggests that we might want to consider possibly looking at a solution to a challenge that does not involve the government, that individual is labeled as heartless and uncaring. They are given a lecture about how the people in question need assistance – as if assistance and government are synonymous terms.

The addiction has moved beyond assistance into control. Instead of dealing with each other, we get the government involved with an ever-growing list of laws and regulations. Some of them grow out of the government bureaucracies, but many of them are initiated at the request of citizens who want the government to deal with whatever situation they are facing.

If we are serious about shrinking Washington, we need to begin by facing our own addictions.

Is there a government program that we participate in, not because we have an urgent need, but just because we "want our piece of the pie"?

Is there a way to deal with an issue using church and community resources instead of a federal program? Have we ever looked for one?

In the beginning, the withdrawal symptoms will be difficult to manage. As with any addict, we will need to begin by facing our own areas of addiction without excuses. We will need to withstand the experience before us without reaching for the government bottle. We will need to learn different ways of dealing with challenges or difficulties. We may even need to stop listening to our fellow addicts who tell that we shouldn't have to abstain until everyone else does.

But if we persevere, we will find that the process gets easier. And just as with every recovering addict, we will find that with God's help we can be free.

Role Models

Americans love sports. Walk through any mall, and you will see kids wearing ball caps with the name of their favorite team, and T-shirts with the name and number of their favorite athlete. There is no other single area which provides so many role models to our children.

Sadly, many professional athletes are better models of spoiled brats than anything else.

But the athletes representing us at the London Olympics are true role models.

Let's start with Michael Phelps, the most decorated Olympian in the history of the games. In his interview with Bob Costas after winning his final medal, he was asked about his first race, in which he placed fourth. Phelps could have made excuses, but he didn't. He said that the results of every race in London, including that first one, were the consequences of his level of training. He said that when he chose his level of training, he was also choosing his level of result. So the greatest swimmer, ever, plainly told every one of our kids that effort matters, even for him.

Now let's talk about gymnast Danell Leyva. He won the bronze medal in the All-Around competition for gymnasts. In his interview, he was asked about his past. His mother brought Danell and his brother from Cuba to the United States when Danell was still a small child. They became American citizens. The interviewer wanted to know if Danell considered himself a displaced Cuban. His response was that he was 100% American, that he was incredibly proud to represent the United States, and that he hoped that with the international attention the Olympics was receiving, some child from the same background as his would see that hope and opportunity still exist in the world. Danell's words and actions are the living embodiment of America's "shining beacon on the hill."

Then there was McKayla Maroney, the American gymnast universally considered the gold standard in Olympic vaulting. In the team competition, her vault left the judges sitting stunned and open-mouthed. But in the individual round, she landed on her bottom on her second vault. Even with that, she won the silver. Afterwards, she was asked if she was dissatisfied with her scores. Her reply was that she was dissatisfied with her performance. She told the reporters that a gymnast who lands on her butt does not deserve to win a gold medal. She had trained as hard as she could for that moment, but when she made a mistake, she admitted it without excuses or whining. She showed our kids how to handle disappointment with grace.

Finally, we have Missy Franklin, the 17-year-old swimmer who won 4 gold medals and 1 bronze, the most any female swimmer has ever won in a single Olympics. In the process she set two world records. She is also an honor student, and swims for her high school team. She comes from Aurora, Colorado, and she told interviewers that she was happy to give the folks back home something to focus on besides the tragic shootings. She had to swim two races with only a 20 minute break. Everyone was worried except Missy. Missy turned out to be correct, as she qualified in the first race, and won a gold medal in the second. When asked, she responded that she just dealt with the situation and did her best. She showed our kids what you can do if you focus on coping instead of complaining.

Happily, these four athletes are the rule, not the exception.

The 2012 U.S. Olympic team is doing us proud, both in the arena and in the limelight. They deserve our congratulations and our thanks for a job well done.

Treating Symptoms

The patient went to his doctor's office complaining of sore throat, swollen glands, headache and fever. The doctor gave him aspirin for the headache and fever, lozenges for his throat, and sent the patient home. A week later, the patient re-appeared and the doctor repeated the treatment. This continued for several months, with the patient coming back every week or two and the doctor addressing the symptoms.

At the end of that time, the patient was rushed to the hospital because the underlying strep infection had developed into rheumatic fever. The patient's family sued the doctor for malpractice, claiming that he had done nothing to stop the disease but had only treated its symptoms.

Everyone knows that America is sick. One of the most obvious symptoms of the illness is economic distress. But economic distress is not the disease.

Consider the following:

The Internal Revenue Service has reported that federal employees and retirees owe roughly $3.4 billion dollars in delinquent taxes.

The Los Angeles Times reported that so many Los Angeles City Hall employees were streaming Olympics coverage online on their office computers that they taxed the system's bandwidth. The city's IT department sent out a memo asking them to stop, out of fear it could trigger a massive computer meltdown. The situation was not unique to Los Angeles.

The Bloomberg News Service obtained a memo that Pentagon Missile Defense Agency Executive Director John James Jr. wrote on July 27, telling DoD government employees to stop using work computers to visit porn sites.

Workers' Compensation Insurance fraud is now so rampant that states have created special departments inside their law enforcement agencies just to investigate and prosecute it. The Pennsylvania Authority has made over 5,800 arrests and gotten court orders for over $53 million in restitution since its creation in 1996. And it's not just Pennsylvania. For example, the Florida insurance fraud authority got court orders for over $47 million in restitution in just the 12 months from July 2011 through June 2012.

Fox News reported on the $17 billion in unemployment insurance fraud, coming from people across the nation who had returned to work, but continued to collect unemployment checks. And that does not include the folks who choose not to even look for work as long as benefits are available.

The list could continue, but we can all see the situation clearly. Every one of these cases has victims. Everyone is paying higher taxes to make up for the fraud in worker's compensation and unemployment. Everyone must deal with more government regulation in as officials attempt to stop the abuse and excess. Everyone pays more for all products and services to make up for the higher costs to business because of the cheating.

With all the higher taxes and extra regulations and higher prices, is it any wonder that there are fewer jobs?

Of course not.

But the taxes and regulations and prices are all just the symptoms of America's disease. The disease itself is not lack of money – it's lack of morals.

And until we stop focusing just on the symptoms and begin treating the disease, we are just as guilty of malpractice as our imaginary doctor, and America's prognosis is just as grim as our imaginary patient's.

Empty Nests

I sent my youngest child to college this week. We hugged good-bye in the parking lot of his dorm, and I watched him walk up to the door. I felt like I was watching him as a six-year-old walking into the school on the first day of first grade. The combination of pride and sadness was almost overwhelming.

His departure means that for the first time in 30 years no children are living in my house. My nest was empty, and the silence seemed to go on forever.

Then my older children began to call. They knew I would be feeling down, and they each took the time to chat.

As I spoke with each of them, I realized that my nest wasn't empty at all. It had just grown.

It is now geographically bigger, since it reaches to each state where one of my children lives. I am still their mom, and I still share their lives. I just do it now through the phone and the Internet. I visit each of them in their homes, and enjoy seeing them as adults.

It is bigger in interests. As each child has become an adult and chosen both career and avocation, I have learned with them. My life and interests have broadened so I can better share their lives, and that experience has been wonderful.

It is also now bigger in population. One of my sons is married to a young woman who has become like a second daughter to me and a second sister to my children. They are about to present our family with the first member of its next generation. Several of my other children are seriously dating lovely young people who now happily attend family events.

It has more branches. I see my children connecting to each other as adults, building their own relationships of caring and support.

I am not unique in this. In fact, I am pretty much average.

It's a cycle that families have followed since the beginning of time. The ties that bind families together aren't limited by a place – they can span any distance. They are not limited by time – they reach across years and span generations.   They are not limited by standards – no one has to be "good enough" to be a member of their own family..

We mostly take families for granted.   We shouldn't.

Over the centuries, governments have come and gone. But the families that lived inside those governments have remained.

Maybe that's because government is an institution created by man, and family is an institution created by God.

The ties that bind families together are exactly like the ties that connect us to the One Who created families. They reach beyond distance and time, allowing for growth and change. They embrace every single one of us with the knowledge that whatever challenges we face, we are never alone.

I spent the summer dreading this moment. Now that it is here, I realize that my nest isn't empty at all. It may not be located at just my address any more, but the love and joy that existed inside that nest are all still there, and will continue to be there in the years ahead.

Instead of an empty nest, I have one that is, and shall always be, full.

Gnats and Camels

If you follow the topics that people seem to get most upset about on social networking and major media outlets, you would think that we live in a nearly perfect world.

For example, there is a huge outcry about some Hollywood actress who sent out a Tweet on Twitter to forward a message hoping that hurricane Isaac would wash all the pro-life Republicans out to sea where they would drown. Admittedly, it is a hateful message.

But the actress can't actually make the hurricane do anything, so the message has no real implications. Why are we so upset about what some actress thinks? She is a person whose job is to play pretend. She isn't really any of the people she has pretended to be – and neither is any other Hollywood celebrity. They only have the power to affect us if we give it to them.

And they live in conditions that require them to generate public attention so they can get the next role. If we just ignored them when they sound off on subjects they know absolutely nothing about, the promise of publicity for their stupid statements would vanish.

As citizens, they are certainly entitled to say anything they wish, but we are not required to listen to anything they happen to say. And most of the time, we shouldn't.

Then there is the grand-daddy of stupid statements made by a politician. Why anyone would put the words "legitimate" and "rape" in the same sentence, much less the same phrase, is beyond comprehension. But to turn a moment of stupidity into a national issue is also ridiculous.

The man obviously is not intending to rape anyone, and is not advocating rape. He admitted his gaffe, and apologized for it.

Yes, he said something stupid, and since he is a candidate, the voters in his state will deal with him in the upcoming election.

But to say that the two examples above, and others like them, are more important than the growing hostility between Iran and Israel, or our monstrous national debt, or our stuttering economy is even more stupid.

The reality is that America has real issues to deal with. Issues that require analytical thought and serious discussion and creative solutions. If we don't address and solve them, we might well be looking at the end of the America we know.   That is a scary possibility.

For many of us, it is easier to focus on the latest Twitter explosion than to honestly face the challenges before us. But we aren't helping ourselves by doing so.

There is an old saying about swallowing camels and straining at gnats.

If we are serious about saving this nation of ours, we need to begin dealing with the camels in our midst, and leaving the gnats alone.

Endowed, not Entitled

Once upon a time there were two brothers. The older would, by birthright, inherit all that his father owned. A day came when the older wanted something to eat. He had been outside all day, and was hungry. The younger had a meal already prepared. The older asked the younger to give him the dinner. The younger agreed, on the condition that the older would give up his birthright in return for the free meal. The older took the deal, gave up his birthright, and ate.

Most of us recognize the story. And we scratch our heads at a person who would give away an entire birthright for one meal.

We shouldn't. We are just like him.

America was founded on the recognition that each of us has a birthright of endowed and unalienable rights. Like all birthrights, it brings the promise of opportunity and blessing, provided that we honor the responsibility of protecting and cherishing it. Our birthright cannot legitimately be taken from any of us, but each of us can choose to give it away. If enough of us make that choice, the birthright's promise will be lost to all of us.

Sadly, many Americans _are_ making that choice. They are selling their birthright of endowed rights for the free meal of government entitlements. And like the older brother in the story, they are convincing themselves that their immediate needs are so important that meeting them is worth what they are losing.

They may not even realize that they are selling one thing to get another. But they are.

It is not a coincidence that as the number of government entitlements increases, there is an equal increase in government's assault on our endowed rights. The government is slowly changing its own job description from "protector of endowed rights" to "grantor of entitlements". If it completes the transition, it will also have changed its status from "servant to" to "master of" America's citizens.

Let's look at just one example. The government is marketing an entitlement to health care. Accepting it means allowing the government "entitler" to determine who may receive what treatment at what cost under what conditions, effectively selling the endowed right of life.   And, since the law creating the entitlement says the government's power to make those treatment determinations is not limited to the individuals who have accepted the entitlement, the loss of the endowed right is more universal than the entitlement it has been traded for. Every American will be affected by the fact that some Americans have decided to sell their birthright.

The younger brother understood the value of the birthright, and he was willing to give something to get it. He understood that the meal would quickly end, while the birthright would last forever.

His elder freely chose immediate satisfaction over long-term blessing.

Today's government also understands the value of our birthright. To get us to trade it away, that government has created a whole system of enticements, hoping that we will act like the older brother -focus only on the meal and forget what we are selling. So far, the tactic is proving to be successful.

The reality is, we can either be endowed, or we can be entitled. An America where endowed rights are cherished will be free and prosperous forever, while an America full of entitlements will last about as long as the older brother's meal. We all know what we think about that older brother. The question is, what do we want our children to think when they remember us?

One Life

My father died this past Sunday. He wasn't rich or famous. He never held an elected office. Most of the world didn't even notice his passing.

But my Dad changed the world.

He was a man who didn't just believe in his faith, he lived it. He was honorable in his business dealings. Every person who dealt with him learned what it was like to actually work with a man of his word. To work with him, they had to live up to that same standard. So honor became a habit and not just a word.

He was generous with his time and his finances. He never asked to have his name on a building, or engraved on a monument. But every one of his gifts changed the life of another for the better, and each of their changed circumstances changed other lives. His generosity is like the waves a pebble makes when it is thrown into a pond – the pebble may disappear, but the waves just keep reaching out until the entire pond is changed.

He was a man who openly and completely loved his wife, at every moment of their marriage. He and my mother still held hands after 55 years as husband and wife. His example taught his children and now his grandchildren that it is not only possible, but wonderful, to keep the vows of marriage. And he left behind children who all have intact marriages.

He cherished life. He welcomed every child as a gift from God Himself. He communicated that love to all he met. His four children gave him a combined 21 grandchildren, and he was as thrilled with the youngest as he was with the oldest. Every one of those grandkids knows what it feels like to be considered a blessing. And they will bring that knowledge with them into their own adult lives.

He was a true feminist. He had four daughters, and although he used to joke about his "harem", he challenged each of us to reach for our dreams.   He made each of us know that we were special because of our femininity, not in spite of it.

He believed in work. Dad set his standards high, and he expected us to meet them. But he stood behind each of us every single step of the way, and when we stumbled, he was the first one to pick us up, dust us off, and get us to try again.

Dad wasn't perfect. Nobody is.

But he was a man who met his life head on, with courage and integrity and love. And now he has gone to be with the God he served for 80 years.

The world would say that Dad's life was ordinary. The world would be wrong.

I would say that I will miss him, but the reality is that his presence will continue to bless my life forever. It is my deepest desire to honor that blessing every day.

Non-Constitutional Rights

On September 17, 1787, 39 Americans signed their names to a legal document. The words of that document were argued throughout the country as their fellow citizens decided whether or not they would accept the structure of government it contained.

When the discussion finally ended, the document was accepted and the United States Constitution became the foundation on which this nation would build, and maintain, a government.

But the Constitution is NOT the founding document of this nation. And when those 39 men signed their names, they included language to prove that they recognized this fact. The final paragraph of the Constitution states:

"done in Convention by the Unanimous Consent of the States present the Seventeenth Day of September in the Year of our Lord one thousand seven hundred and Eighty seven and of the Independance of the United States of America the Twelfth In witness whereof We have hereunto subscribed our Names,"

The Constitution was adopted in what its authors recognized as the twelfth year in the life of the United States of America. So, if 1787 was the twelfth year in the life of this nation, what was the first year? When did the United States actually begin?

In 1776.

There was a document signed in that year as well. And the authors of the Constitution recognized that the words of the 1776 document were actually the ones that birthed this nation.

The distinction matters.

America was founded on the premise that each person has unalienable, or God-given, rights. These rights lie outside of the legitimate reach of any government. If any government attempts to violate these rights, its actions make resistance, and even revolution, justifiable.

The 1776 document defines those unalienable rights. Life, so no government can legitimately remove from any person the right to his own existence. Liberty, so no government can legitimately decide to arbitrarily enforce or ignore the law depending on who is standing before Lady Justice. Pursuit of Happiness, so no government can legitimately dictate the life decisions of its citizens.

Since these rights come from our Creator, they are non-negotiable. The only reason that government legitimately exists is to protect them.

The Constitution is, in modern terms, the "How To" manual for the Declaration. It created a structure of government that its authors believed would best honor the legitimate purpose of government – protecting the unalienable rights of its citizens. The Constitution can be amended. Unalienable rights cannot. And that fact is exactly why those rights are not listed in the Constitution.

The Bill of Rights was designed to outline specific behavioral prohibitions that its authors hoped would keep the government from stepping over its limits. But the Bill of Rights is as amendable as the rest of the Constitution.

The men who gave us the Constitution were wise. Not only did they create a system that limits the federal government, they kept the things that a government cannot legitimately touch out of the language of the document that set up the government.

But they reminded us that the proper definition of the purpose of government had been given to us, and told us where to look to find it. So in their honor, let us do so right now:

We hold these truths to be self-evident, that all men are created equal, that they are endowed by their Creator with certain unalienable Rights, that among these are Life, Liberty and the pursuit of Happiness.--That to secure these rights, Governments are instituted among Men, ...

And now that we have remembered, let us work to uphold and defend.

Redefining Morality

The young woman was dating a very nice guy. They had gotten past first impressions and the fun-filled entertainment that fills the time in new relationships, and were beginning to talk about worldviews and possible permanence.

He was a smoker and she was not.

She actively practiced her faith and he did not.

The couple didn't discuss smoking, but did spend many hours in conversation about the importance and effect of faith, or its lack, on their future lives. In the end, he decided that he did not want to become an active participant in a faith-filled life. In response, she opted not to continue pursuing a permanent relationship with him.

Both of them were comfortable with their decisions, and they have remained friends. Her friends were appalled.

They could not understand how she could have tolerated his smoking. They told her that they could never be with someone who smoked, and that breaking up with a fellow over cigarette use was not only acceptable, but desirable.

But when she shared the fact that they had chosen not to move forward into a deeper relationship because of their different perspectives on the role of faith in their lives, her friends openly stated that she was being absolutely unreasonable, and that if she stuck to that decision, she would find herself alone – forever.

So faith is open to compromise, but smoking isn't.

Welcome to the new morality.

There has been much debate over the effect of removing God from the public marketplace. This is the generation that has grown up in schools where God's name could not be mentioned, and the role of Christianity in creating western civilization could not be acknowledged. If the Church was referred to at all, it was always the villain in the story.

The textbooks were full of the Richelieu's and devoid of the Maximilian Kolbe's. Those whose lives were informed by faith were presented as intolerant, regressive, and mean.

At the same time, being physically healthy and attractive was touted as the ultimate good. And while being healthy is certainly a "good", and there is nothing wrong with taking care of one's appearance, the final result of defining ultimate good in physical terms instead of spiritual ones robs us of the most important part of ourselves.

Many members of the young adult generation reflect the results of that robbery. Suicide rates among young people are alarmingly high; STD infection rates are rising annually; the number of teens being treated for depression is increasing; and self-destructive behaviors like cutting and anorexia are becoming more prevalent.

Can these trends be linked to the diminishing role of faith in the lives of our young people? MTV decided to find out if there was a common thread to happiness. They conducted a survey of young people, asking them if they were happy and then asking what factors were most important in their lives. They were stunned to learn that those who ranked faith as a major factor were twice as happy as those who didn't. They could offer no explanation for this surprising result.

They should have consulted St. Augustine, who discovered and wrote, nearly 1600 years ago, that our hearts were made for God, so we would only be happy when we rested in Him. It's not a new truth – it's a lost one.

For the sake of our children, it's time we find it again.

Definitions

It's not always enough to use the same words.

Comedians pepper their routines with the double meanings that the same words can have. English-language students often stumble over the fact that words do not mean what they appear to be saying. In these cases, we all enjoy the mix-up.

Sometimes, the difference between words and meanings is more serious. Marriage counseling often revolves around the fact that although the spouses are saying the same words, they are not actually meaning the same thing. The counselor's role is to find the misunderstanding and create real communication.

But what happens when there is such a disconnection between the words and the meanings, and there is no counselor?

That is often the case when the citizen deals with the government. And it's why the conversations so often end in frustration and anger.

Let's consider taxes.

The traditional definition of "tax" is the mechanism by which the government is funded. The funding may have come from the citizens, or from some other source. But the word, "tax", meant nothing more than a funding stream.

If you asked most citizens to define "taxation", that is the definition they would give you.

But the government has a very different definition of taxation. In the eyes of the government, taxes are the mechanism by which they can control the behavior of citizens. The government uses taxes to redistribute wealth, to reward or punish the location of a business enterprise, to direct personal and commercial spending decisions, and to stimulate or curtail behavior.

There has never been a conversation about the radical difference in these definitions. In fact, the government has changed the definition through a series of actions that were designed NOT to excite a challenge on the part of citizens. And it has been successful.

Businesses choose locations based on tax incentives, instead of market analysis. And the result is industries that relocate to new communities to get the next tax break, instead of building roots in one place. Companies hire employees who bring 6-month tax amnesties, and fire them at the end of the period so they can hire the next batch of 6-month tax breaks, instead of investing in long-term employees.

Citizens make decisions about preparing for retirement based on tax incentive programs, changing how and where they save their money. People buy cars, homes, and renovations based on the language of tax codes.

Through taxes, the government has also redefined how its citizens interact with the state. We now ask for permission, through the removal of a tax or the creation of an incentive, to do the thing we wish to do. And if we do not receive that permission, we do not act.

We are no longer sovereign citizens, we are the hired help.

In all the discussion about taxes taking place today, no one is challenging the fact that the state has changed the underlying definitions. And unless we do, we will never get real tax reform. Changing a rate in one of the myriad of taxes which we now pay is not changing the system.

And it's the system that is broken.

Fixing it means starting with the correct definition of taxation, and then eliminating any tax or bureaucracy that does not adhere to that definition. If we citizens are serious about restoring our heritage of freedom, we should accept no "solution" that does not begin from that correction.

Do You Know What Your Problem Is?

Any mechanic will tell you that the first step in fixing something is to correctly identify the reason for the problem. If you try to solve the wrong problem, your actions not only won't fix the original situation, they might even make matters worse.

We all know this. It's why we look for the mechanic who can listen to the funny noise and accurately tell us why our car is making it.

So, why aren't we doing the same thing when we look at the situation in America today?

We are told that America has a debt problem and a jobs problem. If we could just get rid of the debt and create more jobs, everything would be fine. And it is certainly true that America has a monstrous debt and unacceptable levels of unemployment.

But are the debt and the unemployment the reason for the situation in America today, or are they the result of the reason?

Consider the following – all true examples of the behavior of Americans today.

John was injured. He required surgery and then rehab. He was absolutely open about the fact that he was going to stay on worker's compensation as long as he possibly could, and was not planning to go back to work until his benefits had all been exhausted.

This is not a financial problem – it's a character problem. Something we used to call Honor is missing.

Harry owns a small manufacturing business. He wanted to hire a few people. He was paying between $10 and $15 an hour for a full-time entry level position in the shop. He couldn't hire anyone because the applicants told him that their unemployment benefits had not yet run out, and they could make almost as much money staying home, so they were not interested in working.

They did ask him to keep them in mind for when their benefits were exhausted.

This also is a character problem. Something we used to call Self-Respect is gone.

Tom owned a business. He enrolled in a government program in which the government subsidized 50% of the salary of a worker who was hired from the welfare rolls for the first 6 months of the worker's employment. He hired a single mother who was trying to attain financial independence. She received outstanding evaluations. At the end of the 6 months, Tom told her that she was being terminated. When she asked why, she was told that the 6-month subsidy had expired, so she was being replaced by another worker who could be subsidized. The mother could not re-apply for assistance for herself and her little one for 6 weeks, so she would have no income at all during that period.

Another character problem. This time it's Justice that has disappeared.

There are many more such stories, and the common thread is a lack of character that creates a financial problem.

No one wants to talk about that. It seems that it is easier to look in our wallets than it is to look in our mirrors.

But until we do, we won't solve anything. We can't solve a character problem with a fiscal wrench. It's like trying to muffle the strange noise our car is making instead of dealing with the broken part. The car will still be broken.

Ask any good mechanic.

Fatal Errors

In the early days of computers, everyone had to use command prompts to accomplish their task. If you gave an impossible command, the computer would flash the words, "Fatal Error" in big red letters on the screen and the entire program would stop. The computer was protecting itself from the incompetence of the operator by keeping that operator from taking another step in a direction that could potentially destroy the entire hard drive.

In order to proceed, someone with the proper authorization codes had to override the warning and make the necessary corrections before the computer would go back online. Sometimes the only possible correction was to restart the entire system.

We need those flashing red letters now.

In the Vice-Presidential debate, we discovered that the American embassy in Paris has an entire detachment of Marines guarding it to ensure the safety of our ambassador and the rest of our delegation. The embassy in Benghazi had no such protection.

The Obama administration has been trying to sell the story that the reason is because the Republican House would not provide more funds.

This is, to use the Vice-President's favorite word, malarkey.

The issue at hand is not how much money the administration had to work with, the issue is how they chose to allocate the resources at their disposal.

It's the kind of budget decision that every one of us makes every single day. We look at what we need, and then decide how to spend what we have based on the relative importance of each item on our list. We may need new tires for the car, and new curtains for our windows. We can only afford one, so we purchase the tires because safety is more important than appearance.

The Obama administration needs to ensure the safety of our foreign delegations.   They decided that it was more important to put our Marines in Paris than in Libya, so they spent the funds they had based on that decision.

With that decision, they are telling us that they considered the situation in Paris to be so much more dangerous than the situation in Libya that they had to deny Marine protection to Libya to send an entire detachment to Paris.

The Americans in Libya knew that they were in danger. In fact, they were flashing big red letters across the State Department's screen over and over again. But the administration's State Department used its authority and overrode the warnings.

This is not a funding problem – this is a judgment problem.

And those judgment errors literally WERE fatal because four Americans were brutally murdered.

Any administration that allocates more resources to protect to Paris than to protect Libya is beyond "correcting". It needs to be shut down, as soon as possible.

This November we have the opportunity to do just that. It's time to end the Fatal Error that is commonly known as the Obama Administration. No other American should have to pay the ultimate price for their incompetence.

The Real Question

What lies at the center of our society?

American society has traditionally been centered around the family, defined as those related by blood, marriage, or adoption. This definition has been both flexible enough to allow for two-parent, single-parent, blended, and extended families, and stable enough to survive the challenges of life.

Family members are bonded by love and respect and commitment. Those bonds are considered unbreakable, so members can experience unconditional love and acceptance. Those bonds cross generational and ethnic lines, span time and distance, and do not recognize economic classes. They allow for individual movement and growth while providing family members with a constant home base to which they can return for refuge, assistance, advice, and encouragement.

When a crisis occurs, family members pull together to face it. Each member supplies his or her individual gift, whether that is wisdom, time, or financial support, in a shared effort to deal with the situation. Members do not measure the amount of help each provides, and do not stop their efforts at an arbitrary cut off point – they remain focused and committed until the situation has been resolved.

Families prepare their members for independence. Children grow up knowing that they will leave their parents' homes to begin the cycle of life and love once again.

Families acknowledge a higher power. They understand the worth and value of each member, from the youngest to the oldest; and they recognize that they are the custodians, not the Creator, of life. Most families pray together, asking the Creator for His blessing and assistance, and thanking Him for answering those prayers.

If society were viewed as an old-fashioned wagon wheel, with a central hub and spokes out to the rim, families would be a bright center to the wheel. They generate life – both biological and economic, which flows from them into the larger society. Family members produce and consume goods and services. They accumulate wealth, which they pass on to future generations, ensuring continued economic life.

Families feed the societies where their centrality is recognized and supported – to the benefit of both the family and the society.

But in the new social order being promoted in America today, family is being replaced by government as the central unit of society.

Under this structure, family is defined as any group of people who come together in a supportive environment, however temporary that group may be. The traditional family ties of blood, marriage or adoption would either be discarded or diluted to allow for any group of individuals to self-define as a family.

In this structure, individuals would be connected to the government. Government ties people to it through conditions of dependence and regulation and ignorance. People do not bond to the government, so they must be tied to it. These conditions create that tie.

Government programs and policies separate the members of a family from each other. Then the state can put barriers between them, creating isolation and forcing each individual to work directly with the state. Government is not compassionate, so individuals must deal with the might of the state when problems arise, even if "might" is not the most appropriate response to the problem.

Government does not acknowledge a higher power. In a society where government is the central entity, the state seeks to prevent citizens from recognizing a divine Creator. Hence, in every major confrontation between believers and non-believers, the "theology" of the non-believers prevails.

In the wagon wheel analogy, government is a dark center. It produces no life. It creates no goods or services. It generates no wealth. Instead, it pulls life and wealth from the larger society down the spokes of the wheel with an insatiable appetite.

In a government centered society, the government will eventually devour everything in its ever-increasing reach – destroying itself and the larger society in the process.

So, do we want to be the center of America's society to be the family or the government?

America's future will be determined by our answer to that one, central question.

Necessary Blindness

During one of the Presidential debates, the moderator asked the candidates where they stood on illegal immigration. He followed up on his question by asking them if they would therefore deny emergency medical care to a 5-year-old child who was injured while in this country illegally.

His question uncovered the unavoidable conflict that occurs when the arbiter of justice is also the dispenser of charity.

Justice is based on law. In a free society, the law must be applied equally to every person. Each of us, regardless of our circumstances, must be held to the same standards of reward and punishment. The image of Lady Justice in her blindfold reminds us that no one is considered to be above, or below, the law's dictates.

The government is the arbiter of justice.

Charity, on the other hand, is based on individual circumstances. To be effective, charity must actually look at the individual person to see what the recipient needs, how best to meet the need, and, if possible, how to move that recipient to a state of self-sufficiency. Charity is guided by standards, but it is based on love and generosity and compassion. To put it briefly, charity has to see.

Traditionally, the church has been the dispenser of charity.

But in the past four decades, the government has usurped the church's charitable mission.

So the blind arbiter of justice is simultaneously acting as the seeing dispenser of charity. No wonder things are a mess.

Putting a blindfold on charity has resulted in rigid eligibility standards that ignore individual circumstances, with the insane result that the difference between the government's "rich" and the government's "poor" is one single penny. That rigid standard destroys initiative because recipients are punished for moving toward independence – unless they can attain it in one giant step. It has taught people that it is easier, and safer, to remain safely below that cut-off point, turning a short term need for assistance into a long-term condition of dependence.

On the other hand, putting holes in the blindfold of justice has resulted in unequal application of the law. Once justice moves from equal to unequal , it is not justice. The law cannot be either mean or kind because the law is not emotional. Holes in the blindfold move the law from an impersonal application of equal justice to an emotional roller coaster where feelings override standards. That is not just changing justice, it is destroying it.

The debate question is a prime example. An injured child needs help. That is charity. Charity belongs to the church. So in a medical facility run by a church, an injured child would be helped.

Illegal immigration is a crime. That is justice. Justice belongs to the government. So a person who has committed a crime should be dealt with according to the laws concerning that crime.

When the two are separated, there is no confusion.

The confusion arises because the government has decided to combine the two roles. But no one can both be blind AND see. In its attempt, the government has perverted charity and destroyed justice.

Any effort to correct the problem must begin by acknowledging this reality, and then working to correct it.

Thanks for the Fleas

Like most Americans, I have spent a lot of time on my knees, asking God for help with the challenges that members of my family were facing. As each of my kids grew, I prayed with them as well as for them because I wanted them to build a relationship with their eternal Father.

It used to be that my desire to make prayer a part of my children's daily lives was supported by the official institutions of America. But that is no longer true. Even Thanksgiving is no longer presented in America's public schools as a holiday based on prayer.

So, what's a mother to do?

I could get angry, or sarcastic, or discouraged. Instead, I looked at other times in history where God was told by the establishment that He was not welcome. One such time happened less than 100 years ago, in Nazi Germany.

In her book *The Hiding Place*, author Corrie ten Boom describes how she and her family hid Jews from the Germans. They eventually got caught and were sent to various concentration camps. Corrie and her sister stayed together and one cold winter night arrived in a new camp. They were dumped into a barracks and told to find a bed.

The beds in that barracks were long rows of boards filled with straw built into narrow tiers. They had to climb up the tiers until they found an empty spot and crawl into the straw. There were no blankets. The sisters tried to burrow into the straw to get a bit of warmth. Suddenly, they both jumped to the floor in disgust.

The straw was filled with hungry fleas.

Corrie began to cry, but her sister took her hands and told her that they were going to say a prayer praising God.

"Even for the fleas?!" Corrie exclaimed.

"Even for the fleas," her sister answered calmly.

Corrie looked into her sister's eyes and couldn't let her down. So she and her sister held hands in that cold and dark and horrible place and thanked God for all His gifts – even the fleas. In the book, Corrie tells her readers that she really didn't mean the words as she said them.

Time went by, and the sister became too ill to join the work crews. She remained in the barrack, knitting socks for the soldiers. When Corrie returned to the barrack that night, her sister told her how the women in that barrack had spent the day praying together and how wonderful it had been. Corrie didn't believe her.

But every day, the same thing happened. The women prayed through the day. Finally, Corrie asked a guard if her sister's reports of prayer were true. The guard confirmed the story.

"How is that possible? The commandant would never allow prayer," Corrie said.

"Oh, the commandant never goes into that barrack," replied the guard.

"Why not?"

"Because it's full of fleas," shrugged the guard.

So, on this Thanksgiving, as I look around at an American establishment that is increasingly hostile to God, I know that as long as I continue to offer a place to Him in my life and in the lives of my children, He will find a way to take my offer. Even if it means I see a few fleas.

That knowledge is something to be thankful for.

Happy Thanksgiving!

The Unnamed Holiday

Welcome to the 2011 Unnamed Holiday Season!

We will shop for Unnamed Holiday gifts. Our children will participate in public school Unnamed Holiday concerts celebrating snow, sleigh bells, and red-nosed reindeer, and then enjoy an Unnamed Holiday break. Municipalities will decorate with Unnamed Holiday trees, wreaths, bells, and maybe a life-sized Santa Claus complete with elves. Some retailers will again order their employees to offer only Unnamed Holiday greetings to customers. And of course there will be an undetermined number of court battles to force more Americans to Unname the holiday before us.

The situation would be amusing if the stakes were not so high. Unfortunately, the stakes could not be higher.

The argument given by the "Unnamers" is always framed as a Separation of Church and State civil rights issue. In reality, it has nothing to do with any particular Church. The goal is not keeping the State separate from a particular denomination. The goal is Separation of God and State. Americans as individuals may believe in a Deity, but that belief should have no place in the public arena. In the public arena, the secular State should be the final authority.

This has nothing to do with protecting individual civil rights and everything to do with expanding the power of the State. It is a fundamental shift in the fabric of our culture.

How can we be "endowed by our Creator with unalienable rights", if we cannot publicly acknowledge a Creator, whose authority is higher than the State's? If there can be no acknowledgement of a power higher than the state, how can we as citizens have been endowed with unalienable rights at all?

If there are no unalienable rights, then the purpose of Government changes from "securing these rights" with the "consent of the governed" to something else. Something defined and controlled by the very Government that was instituted to protect us.

Something that inevitably becomes tyranny.

When Government seeks to grow, it must redefine itself from Servant of the governed to Master. Step One in that redefinition is removal of competitors. Hence, the Unnamed Holiday.

Everyone knows that one does not have to be Christian to celebrate the birth of Christ. He is the most pivotal figure in human history. Even our calendar is based on him. The celebration is a birthday party with a universal invitation to participate at whatever level an individual desires. And for two centuries Americans of all religious beliefs celebrated in joy and fellowship.

It's not the birth of Christ that is the problem. It is the Person. He taught us the truths that this country is founded upon – that there is a divine and almighty Creator, that our rights are unalienable because they come from Him, that Government was instituted to protect those rights, and that Government is answerable to both that Creator and the governed for its performance in that protection.

Two centuries ago, a group of gifted and courageous men, with "a firm reliance on Divine Providence", sacrificed all they had to give us a society based on those truths. Without the recognition of His existence and His authority, we will not preserve that society.

In that spirit, let me be the first to wish you a Merry Christmas!

Yes, Virginia

Years ago, a little girl named Virginia O'Hanlon wrote to the editor of the New York Sun asking if Santa Claus was real. His answer, which spoke of skeptical men in a skeptical age who only believed in what they could see, is as relevant today as it was when Frank Church wrote it.

The name and face of Santa has been plastered over advertising, billboards, movies and television. We have single Santa's looking for wives, reluctant Santa's trying to escape their destinies, drafted Santa's to replace one who is "retiring", and even bad Santa's. The stories all have happy endings, with the magic of the North Pole somehow saving the day.

None of them are real, and many of them are even distasteful. Thankfully, none of them is Santa, either. Because Saint Nicholas, like every saint, is real.

He was born in Asia Minor and was bishop of the town of Myra in the fourth century. When he died he was buried in the cathedral there. When the Saracens conquered Myra in the early eleventh century, his remains were moved to the Italian city of Bari in 1087. His tomb is visited by thousands every year, even to this day.

His bones exude a clear liquid, called the "manna of Saint Nicholas", which is extracted from the shrine every year on May 9 in a formal ceremony conducted by the Rector of the Basilica in Bari, in the presence of the delegate of the Pope, the Archbishop of Bari, an Orthodox Bishop, civil authorities, the local clergy and the faithful. This has happened every year since 1980. The manna is distributed and is considered a relic with healing properties.

Nicholas is the patron saint of children, Russia, Greece, Sicily, sailors, prisoners, bakers, and pawnbrokers. His image is second only to Mary's in religious icons of both the Eastern and Western churches.

The stories of his generosity and kindness are legendary.

Santa Claus is a translation of his name.

When our children are little, we tell them to "ask Santa" at Christmas time. They can ask for anything – without limit. All Santa wants in return is goodness.

Isn't that exactly how we are supposed to relate to God?

But God is bigger than anything that we can comprehend. Developing an effective and complete relationship with God is the work of a lifetime. A work which most of us do not finish before our time here is done. That is why He sent His Son – so we would have someone we COULD connect with.

Saint Nicholas is a person who made that connection. When people pretend to be Santa, they act with levels of generosity and charity and kindness that they do not normally exhibit. In other words, they get closer to God. In doing so, they discover happiness.
And even in the convoluted versions of Santa being pushed by today's secular media, that message of happiness through goodness continues to resonate.

Yes, Virginia, there is a Santa Claus. He is not just an idea. He was, and is, a saint. A saint who reminds us that we are loved without limits. A saint who challenges us to remove the limits on how we love others. A saint who calls us to holiness as we prepare to celebrate the greatest gift mankind has ever received.

And all we have to do is follow his example.

For Unto Us

They are among the most well-known words ever spoken. Most of us will smile when we hear them, and complete the phrase in our minds. We will see a stable, and a star, and shepherds, and hear the voices of angels.

The event in that stable changed the world.

By today's standards, it shouldn't have. After all, there was no one from the government in attendance. There was no one of wealth. In fact, there was no one the world would have considered to be important at all.

There was, however, a family.

A family in which the husband and the wife loved God and each other.

The wife in that family had trusted in the depth and strength of her husband's love for her when she had agreed to the request brought to her by the angel. She knew that he would hold her life and the life of her unborn Child in his hands; that a single word from him would result in her death by stoning.

The husband had never said that word. Even when he had not understood the entirety of what was happening before his eyes. His love for her was unconditional, so he had decided to sacrifice his own reputation to protect her. And it was only after he had chosen self-sacrifice that the complete reality of the Child was revealed to him.

It was the marriage that created the situation for the Child to be born. The world was changed because a man and a woman honored the covenant that was, and is, marriage.
The power of that covenant is as real today as it was two thousand years ago.

We are a society that is struggling with a myriad of potentially devastating problems. The list is nearly endless.

If we are serious about solving them, we need to look at the single best method for dealing with all of them. A method that does not involve a new government entitlement program, or a thousand page law, or another federal agency.

We can each work to strengthen our own family.

We can deepen the bonds between ourselves and our spouses. We can strengthen our communication with our children. We can reach out to older relatives. Perhaps such efforts will mean that we must practice forgiveness or patience. Perhaps they will demand extra time or finances. Perhaps they will challenge us to reach past our own comfort zones.

We will be in good company.
The young woman who bore the Child we celebrate, and the husband who loved her enough to trust in what he could not see, have shown us what is possible when we love God and each other.
If we truly desire to receive the gift of love that they gave us, the best way to do so is to follow in their footsteps.

I Believe

It was the centurion's last duty station. In less than a month, he could return to Rome and his family. On this Friday, he had been assigned to the execution detail. It was an unpleasant duty, but at least it was quiet.

So he was shocked at the mob coming up the hill, screaming and shouting at a Man who looked like he would not live to receive his final punishment. The centurion quickly had his men form a circle around the execution site, blocking the approach of the crowd once the man had arrived.

The soldiers performed their duty, and the cross was raised. As the centurion looked up into the face of the Man on the cross something seemed familiar. He quickly turned away.

Then a woman approached, supported by a young fellow and two female companions. The young one asked the guards if the group might approach the cross. The centurion heard the guard refuse, saying that there was no room. He turned at the words, and the woman's eyes found his.

And suddenly he was three decades younger, standing in a raucous inn in a town called Bethlehem. He had been a new recruit then, and had been so excited to go to a distant land to conduct the Emperor's census. The excitement had been short-lived. The tiny village had no entertainment, so the soldiers had taken over the courtyard of the inn, drinking and carousing into the wee hours every night. He had never been a big drinker, so he usually sat by the wall until it got quiet enough to sleep.

He had been sitting there when he noticed the innkeeper open the door that night. A young man stood in the doorway, gesturing back into the street. The soldier looked where the man pointed, and saw a woman sitting on the back of a donkey. Her condition was unmistakable.

The innkeeper took one glance at the woman, paled, and firmly told the man that there was no room for him or his wife. The soldier saw the wife's eyes as the innkeeper began to close the door. He had expected to see anger and fear and disappointment in those eyes, but instead they smiled at her husband with love and trust and serenity.

He couldn't believe those eyes.

And now, he began to worry about the woman herself. He told himself that it was none of his concern, but he couldn't let it go. So, after arguing with himself for a few minutes, he stood and slipped out the door of the inn. He began walking the streets, starting at one end of the village and working his way toward the other.

That was when he saw the group of shepherds. They all seemed to be looking up and listening to something. The soldier quietly fell in behind them.

They walked to the outskirts of the town, and began entering a stable.

The soldier moved toward the door, and stopped. There was the woman. She was just laying a newborn Child into a manger.

The soldier didn't know how she knew that he was there but she turned and smiled at him, inviting him with her eyes. And suddenly he, a tough new centurion, was afraid. He knew that if he entered that stable, he would never be the same. He began to back away silently.

Her eyes sadly watched him leave.

He had never seen her again – until now. She was standing in front of his guard, trying to reach the Man on the Cross.

The old centurion ordered the guard to let the woman and her companions into the circle. He followed her to the foot of the cross, standing quietly just behind her.

She turned and gazed at him with the same invitation in her eyes, the invitation that he had rejected over 30 years before.   This time he accepted it, and looked fully into the face of the Man on the cross – her Son.

It had taken him over 30 years, but he realized that he had finally entered the stable where Love was born.

"Truly, this is the son of God," he said.

Merry Christmas!

We Will Build This Nation

We are about to enter one of the most important election years this nation has ever experienced. And while our participation is critical, it is also vital to remember that the strength of this nation does not reside in the halls of any capital.

It will continue to flow from the same sources that built America as long as we preserve them.

On this eve of a new year, let us take a moment to recognize those sources, and resolve together to hold and strengthen them in the days ahead.

This is a nation built on faith, on a collective acknowledgement that the government is answerable for its conduct to a higher authority, that legal is not always synonymous with right, and that right is the standard which we must always seek to follow.

This is a nation built on family, on the knowledge that the love, courage, commitment and fortitude to honor marriage vows, raise children, and care for each other at every stage of life create the very backbone of our country.

This is a nation built on opportunity, on a recognition that success can belong to those who are willing to work for it no matter what their backgrounds may be, that it is possible to actually turn the dream of achievement in its reality.

This is a nation built on personal responsibility, on facing the fact that our behavior does have consequences that we must face, that freedom means we face our failures as well as our successes.

This is a nation built on community, on developing the ties that bind us to each other so we can work together to solve the problems and meet the needs that would conquer any one of us alone.

This is a nation built on generosity, on reaching out to those in need with the help and support necessary to help them meet the challenge of the moment and move past it.

This is a nation built on thrift, on the certain knowledge that living within one's means is the safest path to security, and that there is a value in saving for tomorrow.

This is a nation built on education, on the reality that we can only preserve our heritage if we know and understand it, and that climbing the ladder of opportunity begins with knowledge.

This is a nation built on law, where each individual is judged according to conduct instead of status, and no one is outside the boundaries of the law's standards.

These sources built this nation. Like all nations, we have not always perfectly upheld them. But our history has been one of coming closer than any other – ever.

As we read them, we notice that not one of them depends on the government. The government's role is simply to create an environment in which we can practice them freely.

So as we move into this election year, we have two tasks before us. The first is to evaluate each candidate to see if he or she understands, appreciates, and adheres to the qualities that built this nation.

The second, which is simultaneously more important and more difficult, is to look at ourselves with the same evaluative eye, with a willingness to change the areas of our own shortcomings.

America was built by her people, and her future rests in our hands. Let's work to make it a future we can all be proud of.

Finding America

What, exactly, makes this nation "America"?

It's not economics.   Economic conditions are always the result of a nation's culture and policies, not the cause. We need to ask what created the culture and policies that made us the most prosperous nation in history.

The answer tells us what we, as a nation, believe. Our Founders began by saying, "We hold these truths to be self-evident".

Our entire history flows from our belief in those self-evident truths.

In modern language, the truths of America's heritage are:

God exists and is the highest authority. The American Revolution can only be justified if there was an authority above the King – an authority whose standards the King was violating. A government can only be wrong if there is something higher to measure its actions against.

Our Creator is the source of our unalienable rights. If there is no Creator, we are not endowed. We can only have whatever the government decides to give us. And what a government gives, a government can take. For rights to be unalienable, they must be beyond the reach of the government.

The voice of the church is a necessary part of a free society. It doesn't matter what denomination, the presence of the church is a constant reminder to everyone that the government is not the final answer.

There are legitimate limits on the power of the state. If there is an authority above the state, and there are individual rights beyond its reach, then there must be limits on what the state is allowed to do. The United States Constitution clearly defines those limits.

The government is accountable to the people for its conduct. Government is the entity that the people establish to protect their unalienable rights. Since the people establish the government, the government is accountable to them. This is both a right and a responsibility.

Government functions should be handled at the most local level of government possible. In order for the people to hold the government accountable, every government function should be handled at the most local level possible.

Every person must be treated equally before the law. No one can be above, or below, the standards of the law. No person or group can be above, or below, both its protections and its requirements.

Every person deserves the opportunity to direct his own destiny. No government has the legitimate power to guarantee the success of its citizens, or protect them from their failures.

The fundamental unit of American society is the family. Strong families require the lowest level of government services or interventions; therefore, the most effective way to keep government within its legitimate limits is to preserve and protect the traditional family.

Church and community are the preferred providers of social welfare programs. We do have an obligation to assist those in need. Church and community programs provide that assistance without creating a mentality of entitlement.

There is an American culture, forged from a melting pot of ethnicities, and embraced by generations of settlers who came seeking to become part of this nation. They built the most exceptional nation the world has ever seen.

That is our American heritage. It has been paid for with the lives,
fortunes, and honor of our Founders, and protected with the blood
of generations of our military men and women.

Today, we are its guardians. Let history show that we rose to
defend it!